Securing the Schoolyard

Securing the Schoolyard

Protocols that Promote Safety and Positive Student Behaviors

Nicholas D. Young, Christine N. Michael, and Jennifer A. Smolinski

ROWMAN & LITTLEFIELD

Lanham • Boulder • New York • London

Published by Rowman & Littlefield
An imprint of The Rowman & Littlefield Publishing Group, Inc.
4501 Forbes Boulevard, Suite 200, Lanham, Maryland 20706
www.rowman.com

6 Tinworth Street, London SE11 5AL, United Kingdom

British Library Cataloguing in Publication Information Available

Library of Congress Cataloging-in-Publication Data Available

ISBN 978-1-4758-4850-2 (cloth : alk. paper)
ISBN 978-1-4758-4851-9 (pbk. : alk. paper)
ISBN 978-1-4758-4852-6 (electronic)

Contents

Acknowledgments

With deep appreciation and gratitude, we wish to acknowledge Sue Clark for her skilled editing of this manuscript. Her attention to detail and her well-honed language skills made her an important contributor to this tome. Along with her tremendous professional contributions to our team, Sue has long since become a valued friend.

Preface

Securing the Schoolyard: Protocols that Promote Safety and Positive Student Behaviors sets the stage for schools to consider how best to develop programs and protocols that work in contemporary society to ensure the safety of staff and students. In a world where school violence has received global attention, this book was written to be a valuable resource for all pre-service and veteran teachers, school administrators, higher education faculty, parents, policy makers, law enforcement and security professionals, and all others who have a vested interest in safeguarding all who inhabit our schools every day.

This book provides a review of school safety initiatives worldwide. There is a robust discussion of interventions necessary to combat various kinds of school violence, including the prevalence of cyberbullying and other forms of cyber-violence. Strategies for forming powerful partnerships in prevention through connections with community and local police are discussed. The importance of safety planning and school prevention programs also are stressed. *Securing the Schoolyard: Protocols that Promote Safety and Positive Student Behaviors* is rich with concrete protocols for ensuring school security.

The motivation for writing this book comes from several concerns:

- *Our belief that all students deserve to go to school daily, experience secure and supportive learning environments, and return home safely at the end of the day;*
- *Our concern about the recent escalation in acts of violence that take place inside our classrooms and in the communities that surround them;*
- *Our understanding that there are societal forces, including the prevalence of violence in various media and the round-the-clock presence of social media communications, that have changed the face of acts of school*

*aggression, making cyberbullying and other forms of technological attacks
against students far more likely than in past decades;*
* *Our recognition that schools must form integral partnerships with law
enforcement, including local police, in order to effect security programs
that work;*
* *Our knowledge that there are proven strategies used in other countries that
may prove fruitful in our country's battle against school violence;*
* *Our commitment to viewing schools, families, and community members
as an inextricably linked network in supporting school safety and student
security;*
* *Our belief that each school in our country must engage in safety planning,
articulate clear protocols for dealing with acts of violence, and train all
members of the school community to understand how to implement those
protocols if needed and;*
* *Our years of experience in educating parents, teachers, staff, school counselors, and other helping professionals that has led to the formulation of
best practices in school policy, discipline, law, curriculum, and school
climate that result in secure schools and schoolyards.*

Although the history of school violence is long, going back to the earliest
schools established in this country and around the world, the face of school
violence has changed dramatically. Among the factors influencing the nature
of school security are demographic changes in families, schools, and neighborhoods; the burgeoning role of social media and other technologies in the
lives of our children; a rise in mental health issues among children and adolescents; and challenges to our police forces in terms of the sophistication of
weaponry used in many attacks.

The twenty-first century feels, at times, as though it has been dominated
by school shootings. Ahmed and Walker (2018) note the many school shootings that took place in the first twenty-one weeks of 2018, including those in
Noblesville, Indiana; Santa Fe, Texas; Palmdale, California; Ocala, Florida;
Lexington Park, Maryland; and Birmingham, Alabama. Statistics shows that,
on average, shootings occurred in every geographic area across America
and at all school levels (Ahmed & Walker, 2018; Florida & Boone, 2018).
With these statistics in mind, this book addresses the explosion of school
violence in the United States with the aim of sharing protocols that can result
in increased prosocial behavior and safe classrooms, schoolyards, and other
school-sponsored activities.

School violence and aggression, in general, can be found in ancient and
contemporary settings around the world. Acts of aggression have ranged
from shootings, stabbings, physical and verbal assaults, sexual harassment,
bullying and, early on, running schoolmarms and masters out of their schools;

however, historically, school security was breached infrequently and in isolated fashion.

More recent school violence, unfortunately, exists in many forms including adult on adult, student on student, adult on student, and student on adult. Each leaves the victims scarred in one form or another and puts both groups at greater risk of future violence. This country has made a firm commitment to educate all of its children, yet many face a higher likelihood of encountering some form of aggression against them or will be witness to an act of aggression in the schools. Oftentimes, this violence is rooted in the communities surrounding the schools and, at other times, violence erupts in the schoolyard and spills out into the community. Many experts suggest that seeds of school violence are sown in cyberspace as well.

A key component in school safety is the commitment on the part of educational and community leaders to create protocols that lead to greater security. This involves forming powerful partnerships with law enforcement, especially community police forces, in order to tailor interventions to the needs and concerns of specific neighborhoods and their schools. These initiatives also must be steeped in a clear understanding of how new technologies and weaponry have changed the way in which schools must think about securing their buildings and schoolyards, as well as providing safety for students and their families during extracurricular events.

While it is essential to create programming to bolster the mental and emotional health of our students as a means of preventing school violence, current times require that schools also attend to developing clear, fair, effective, and widely understood protocols to prevent crises when possible, and to react swiftly and professionally in the face of an emergency.

A web search for the definition of "protocol" shows that it is defined as a code of correct conduct (Merriam-Webster, 2018a). Safe, secure schools develop and articulate protocols that range from addressing behavioral issues, academic integrity, honor codes, athletic team policies, and, more recently, attacks upon or within schools or school communities. It is through these protocols that schools can initiate positive change and create academic institutions that value all members.

The focal points of the chapters of *Securing the Schoolyard: Protocols that Promote Safety and Positive Student Behaviors* center on violence prevention, safety planning, international school security programs, the dangers of cyberspace, police partnerships, and specific protocols that work. This tome is a balanced integration of research, theory, proven best practice, and explicit protocols to provide a comprehensive approach to safety and security. The approach gleans much from cross-cultural and media studies, security and community policing, and educational practice and, as such, the book strives to present protocols that all schools can implement.

The authors comprise a team of experienced PK–12 and higher education professionals whose goal is to tackle pressing issues of how to best stem the tide of school and community violence affecting young people and their families. By providing a seminal understanding of some of the current theory and practice behind law enforcement practices, school safety protocols and preparation, supporting school diversity, innovative behavioral interventions, and cross-cultural research on school security programs, the authors hope to disseminate knowledge that can assist stakeholders in creating a safe and secure learning environment where all members can engage in teaching and learning without fear of unnecessary action or reprisal.

Chapter 1

From Grade School to Guns

Violence in American Schools

In a review of K–12 American schools from the time period of 1974–2013, statistics paints a vivid portrait of modern school violence that is characterized by a multitude of issues that affect both the victims and the perpetrators before, during, and after the attacks occur (Lambert 2013; Cox & Rich, 2018). While acts of violence transpire at all school levels, only 10 percent of incidents were reported in an elementary school; yet, 50 percent of these incidents were perpetrated by adult intruders or adults who shot from an off-campus location (Lambert, 2013).

A noticeable difference occurs at the middle and high school levels where adults accounted for only 10 percent of violence, indicating that the vast majority of acts came from within the schools, from students (Lambert, 2013). The majority of all deaths came from gunshot wounds; yet, it is likely that, had a weapon not been available at the time of rage, these incidences might have been avoided (Lambert, 2013).

Accounts from these violent incidents, including witness testimony and diaries, journals, websites, and other social media records by the shooters themselves, indicate that it was relatively easy for the shooter to obtain a weapon from the home, while in other cases, the weapon was purchased by the perpetrator or a friend (Cox & Rich, 2018; Lambert, 2013).

Lambert (2013) found incredible variations among the types of schools that experienced violence, the perpetrators, and the victims. During the forty-year time span reviewed, most violent school deaths were single events, usually the result of some sort of altercation between people, rather than in mass events such as the Columbine shooting (Lambert, 2013). Single events comprised two-thirds of all school violence; the other third was defined by mass violence, threats of mass violence, hostage taking, and guns accidentally

1

going off in school (Lambert, 2013). Other statistics were equally surprising to include

- 75 percent of all school deaths were gun related and 99 percent were mass school violence incidents.
- 10–15 percent of student deaths happened when students were traveling to or from school but were not on a bus or in the school confines.
- 70 percent of all incidents happened in high schools and were carried out by students.
- 48 percent of the on-campus perpetrators were between the ages of 14 and 17.
- 45 percent of violent school incidents occurred in urban areas, 29 percent in suburban, and 13 percent each in rural areas and small towns (Lambert, 2013).

Fortunately, there were many thwarted attempts at school violence. These in-progress attempts most often ended in suicide; surrender or capture by law enforcement; weapon failure and/or running out of ammunition; being tackled by teachers, students, or administrators; or having the situation de-escalated through verbal negotiations (Lambert, 2013; Cox & Rich, 2018).

There are four ways in which a cycle of violence may be perpetuated (Lambert, 2013). The first and foremost way of creating more violence was through revenge. This could be one-on-one, gang or turf-related, or a mass incident, but all shared the commonality of an individual's desire to get back for real or perceived injuries (physical or emotional) to himself or someone close to him (Cox & Rich, 2018).

Copycat incidents were the second way of continuing violence; these were perpetrated by both youth and adult assailants (Lambert, 2013). Incidents that were triggered within atmospheres of heightened tension, anger, or violence were the third category, while strings of events were the last category (Lambert, 2013). In these cases, particular locations seemed to spawn multiple incidents, yet those incidents were tied together geographically, rather than by any direct connection among them. This happened with both homicides and suicides and appeared as though students learned from or were influenced by others around them (Cox & Rich, 2018).

POSSIBLE CAUSES FOR SCHOOL DISTURBANCES

Crews and Counts (1997), authors of one of the most comprehensive books on school disturbances throughout American history, note that there have been a few traditional theories that attempt to explain school violence.

The first of these, arising in the 1700s, centers on the role of human free will. This theory says that individuals act upon their own free will, rationally, when they choose to pursue their aims (Crews & Counts, 1997). If people are free agents, acting hedonistically, it is logical that punishment should be swift and harsh to "unwill" them from acting in such a manner again. Within this theory, there is no consideration of the mental state of individuals as they act, and social factors that might influence their actions are irrelevant.

A second theory, positivism, took hold in the 1800s. Unlike free will theory, positivism emphasized a criminal's personal traits and background (Crew & Counts, 1997). Offenders were viewed as "sick" and their biological, psychological, social, cultural, and physical environments were considered as "treatment" was constructed. Considering environmental factors, theorists such as Merton (1938) looked to the socialization that individuals received, and the concept of "anomie" or disconnection and social isolation were central. As the theory explained, those who felt alienated from social interactions and without support from peers were more likely to become criminals or delinquents (Crews & Counts, 1997).

Thrasher's (1936) "gang theory" postulated that gangs frequently arise from spontaneous play groups. A natural play group can become transformed into a gang if conflicts erupt between groups. In those circumstances, it makes sense for people to band together in a gang for protection. These gangs also may fulfill unmet needs such as security, affiliation, and belonging that might not be fulfilled by family or community or school. By middle adolescence, gangs most frequently have taken on characteristics that distinguish them, such as name, distinctive clothing, racial or ethnic emphasis, and modus operandi (Thrasher, 1936).

The role of behavioral conditioning also was integrated into many theories. Behavioral theorists believed that lifestyle behaviors, including delinquent ones, were taught, not biological (McLeod, 2017). Within intimate personal groups, such as gangs or neighborhoods or families, certain criminal behaviors were learned in interactions with others to include both motivations and techniques for committing crimes (Crews & Counts, 1997).

Another view is that held by biological theorists who view inbred traits, rather than environmental factors, as the explanation for criminal behaviors (McCaghy, Capron, Jamieson, & Carey, 2008). There is a wide range of possible factors—from neurological dysfunctions to emotional disturbances and other mental health problems—that have been seen as likely explanations for delinquent behavior (McCagny et al., 2008). Likewise, there are certain "at risk" personalities that raise the possibility that an individual will commit anti-social acts (McCagny et al., 2008).

Langman (2009) spent a decade studying the mental states of school shooters, searching for mental health clues to their violent behaviors. Contrary to popular belief, the shooters were not loners; though most of them suffered from suicidal thoughts and depression. This was not the trigger that led to the deviant behavior though. While not always mutually exclusive, there are several typologies that exemplify shooters to include traumatized children, schizotypal personality disorders, schizophrenics, and psychopaths.

Commonalities existed between the shooters to include a lack of empathy, emotional distress, suicidal thoughts, existential rage, feelings of victimization, a sense of hopelessness, and extreme reactivity (Langman, 2009). Vulnerable identities led to highly abnormal responses; these overreactions often grew out of accumulated grievances over a number of years and led to self-loathing. For boys—and almost all school shooters are males—shame, envy, and a perceived failure of manhood contributed to rage and depression (Langman, 2009).

The disparity of gun-related deaths among young men in the United States as compared with other developed countries, such as England and Wales, range from 4.5 percent to greater than 50 percent times higher than reported elsewhere (Logue, 2008). Additional statistics suggests that most violent deaths in American schools are firearms-related; the perpetrators are male; and the motive is revenge for some interpersonal dispute or perceived injustice (Logue, 2008).

INEQUITIES AND VIOLENCE

Interestingly, equity issues also seem to have played a part in violent actions. Prevalent in the 1960s and 1970s, violent protests and other actions often came in response to perceived social injustices; yet, these also played a role in crime post-desegregation. As Shen (2013) wrote:

> In the past decade, resegregation through so-called "white flight" and relaxed integration enforcement is leading to greater inequality from an earlier age. Modern inner-city schools are often underfunded, while dropout rates are high, and violence is common. Police officers routinely intervene to discipline students for minor infractions, exposing minority kids early to the criminal justice system. Greater allocation of resources may not be enough to halt the cycle of racially-skewed poverty and crime as long as racial and class segregation continues. (n.p.)

Over fifty years after the *Brown v. Board of Education* decision, integration has helped keep black students from dropping out, while improving their earnings, health, and decreasing incarceration rates (Fisman, 2013). Yet the occurrence of re-segregation within the schools since 2001, when poor black students stopped getting bused to integrated schools, is fast undoing the progress made since the civil rights era (Fisman, 2013).

A study of Charlotte-Mecklenburg schools in North Carolina showed that these schools were considered to be a civil rights battleground after a 1971 Supreme Court decision to allow busing of minority students into white schools (Billings, Deming, & Rockoff, 2012). Prior to 2001, school populations were racially mixed by including some minority neighborhoods not immediately around the school; however, after the halt of mandated busing, the district redrew its school boundaries, leading once again to separating students into mostly black and mostly white schools (Billings et al., 2012).

Several studies echoed the undeniable truth that even with increased funding to minority schools, young black students placed in re-segregated schools were suddenly involved with law enforcement more often (Billings et al., 2012; Johnson, 2011). At the beginning of this century, a young black man was four times more likely to be arrested for a violent offense than a young white man (Fisman, 2013). While that figure may seem shocking to many, it actually represented a tremendous gain since 1969, when the chances of a black male under the age of 18 being arrested for a violent crime was twelve times that of a white man (Fisman, 2013).

While academic parity may have been achieved, and that fact is highly disputed, it was true that a poor black male student was 15 percent more likely to get arrested if attending a school that had 60 percent minority students rather than 40 percent minority (Johnson, 2011; Billings et al., 2012). These findings reinforce the fact that white students did not commit fewer crimes with the end of busing; rather, black students committed significantly more (Fisman, 2013).

While court-ordered integration led to more equitable resources and spending per student regardless of race, poor minority students had access to the same kinds of opportunities as white children (Shen, 2013). In the Charlotte study, increased resources for re-segregated minority schools kept the dropout rate level; however, passive integration policies have not helped students to change their socioeconomic fates (Billings et al., 2012). Several studies tie the racial crime gap directly to segregation and concluded that if additional resources were provided to segregated schools, classroom instruction and course offerings could be improved, but only intentionally integrative student assignment policies could radically impact the racial or socioeconomic backgrounds of students who attend American schools (Johnson, 2011; Billings et al., 2012).

Many scholarly studies highlight the benefits to black students of court-ordered desegregation; for example, Guryan (2004) reported that integration led to a 25 percent decrease in black dropout rates during the 1970s; during this same time, the rate for whites remained unchanged. A 2011 study by

Johnson that looked at the longer-term effects of desegregation on children of the civil rights era showed similar conclusions to include that desegregation led to higher earnings, better health, and a higher likelihood of staying out of prison for black males.

TEACHER VIOLENCE AGAINST STUDENTS

While student violence in our schools tends to receive the most attention in the media, there is a parallel history of teacher violence against students. This violence is rooted in the notion of corporal punishment as a means of deterring student misbehavior or responding to it when it occurs. Hyman and Perone (1998) define corporal punishment as the deliberate infliction of pain in response to an offense, while *Merriam-Webster* (2018b) terms it as "punishment inflicted on a person's body."

Historically, school authorities have seen the necessity of using their power and authority over children if they are to educate them. Not only does an act of corporal punishment address the offender, but it is intended to convey a message to other students. Midlarsky and Klain (2005) make the interesting observation that, in Colonial America, teaching was not considered a valued profession; thus, teachers were rarely trained, had few resources, and were poorly paid. Corporal punishment, therefore, was a necessary teaching tool to force bored students to take part in the mandatory rote learning of required subjects.

During Colonial times a teacher's chief role was to maintain classroom order, not impart knowledge and skills; thus, obedience was essential. They held complete authority over their pupils and repetitively drilled them in religion, morals, and character; those students who did not learn were routinely punished and the community expected such punishment (Midlarsky & Klain, 2005).

Teachers could inflict a wide range of punishments upon their students to include rapping knuckles with rulers, pulling ears, or having to clean up schoolyard trash. If the offense was more serious, teachers might use the pillory or whipping post, while a child who stole could face the branding iron (Midlarsky & Klain, 2005). The selection of potential teachers depended heavily upon their ability to physically handle the older boys, as they often enjoyed beating teachers and running them out of town (Midlarsky & Klain, 2005).

Crews and Counts (1997) note that after the Revolutionary War, even though American citizens earned individual liberty, there was a prevailing national fear that too much liberty could lead the country to anarchy. Education was viewed as the great leveling tool that could mediate tensions between personal freedom and social order. Threats, intimidation, physical interactions, and outright abuse were weapons of choice in maintaining order and attempting to motivate students who were bored and disengaged (Crew & Counts, 1997).

Violence against students was carried out in many forms, and the instruments of such punishment were on full display at most school houses. One might see whipping posts, paddling devices, whips, and other instruments. Teachers also might send students to small, windowless confinement areas known as "dungeons" where they were left for long periods of time. Teachers prided themselves on their punishments and, unless it caused permanent injury, charges of excessive force were never filed. A headmaster, for example,

> *published a list of the finest accomplishments of his career and cited that he administered 911,527 blows with a cane, 124,010 blows with a rod, 20,989 blows with a ruler, 136,715 blows with his hand, 1, 111, 800 raps on the head and ordered 613 kneelings on a triangular piece of wood.* (Midlarsky & Klain, 2005, p. 49)

During the Industrial Revolution, for the first time, children were treated differently from adults due to labor conditions and the first courts specifically to deal with juveniles were created (Crews & Counts, 1997). Mandatory education for all children was born, given the growing need for an educated labor force and, while teachers still could employ corporal punishment, it was to be used only as a last resort (Midlarsky & Klain, 2005). By the 1860s some states had outlawed it altogether, while others forbid its use unless students acted out in a violent manner.

As teaching became more professionalized, violence against students decreased within schools in the modern era, yet as late as 1969, a majority of teachers still believed in the judicious use of corporal punishment, and particularly in the South, paddling and other beatings continued (Crews & Counts, 1997). Hyman and Wise (1979) chronicled one of the worst cases of corporal punishment in which three students who were caught on school grounds with cigarettes were given the choice to either eat the eighteen remaining cigarettes or face paddling; they chose to eat them but developed kidney infections and ulcers after and had to be hospitalized.

In another documented case, a Florida student was beaten for being too slow in leaving the auditorium. He sustained multiple, serious injuries and his father ended up taking the school to court for violating his 8th Amendment rights; however, the Supreme Court of the United States decided that corporal punishment was not a cruel and unusual punishment because it had been used in schools for centuries (Midlarsky & Klain, 2005).

STUDENT VIOLENCE AGAINST TEACHERS

Violence against teachers began with the earliest schools and classrooms. Many students, especially older boys, took great delight in driving off their teachers through acts of aggression (Midlarsky & Klain, 2005). A new term—battered teacher syndrome—captured the physical and psychological scarring that the nation's teachers experienced, resulting in such symptoms as depression, anxiety, illness, eating disorders, disturbed sleep, increased suicide, and other physical and mental health disorders (Bloch, 1977). Yet, even as it became a national crisis, it was "rarely defined, empirically studied, or meaningfully discussed among academic circles" (Espelage et al., 2013, p. 76).

One of the most recent, well-publicized incidents involved a parental assault on a teacher in Pittsburgh, Pennsylvania in which an elementary school teacher was seriously injured with a brick for confiscating a student's cell phone in class (Dupuy, 2017). The mother subsequently was charged with making terroristic threats, stalking the teacher, aggravated assault, and reckless endangerment (Dupuy, 2017).

The teacher, who taught pre–K through eighth grade, had taken the girl's cell phone in accordance with the district's no-cell phone policy (Dupuy, 2017). The fourth grader then bit the teacher and school administration called in her mother. In a meeting with the teacher, the child told her mom that the teacher had choked her. That report apparently enraged her mother, who told the teacher she would "get it later" (Dupuy, 2017, n.p.).

The cost of violence against teachers is severe and includes teacher attrition and absenteeism, lost wages, increased workers' compensation claims, and the loss of instructional time or poor instruction when teachers concentrate on their safety, rather than their craft (Bloch, 1977; Dupuy, 2017). Student learning can be negatively impacted, and school climate affected adversely, not to mention the negative publicity for the schools in which violence takes place (Steffgen & Ewen, 2007).

Medical and mental health costs skyrocket when teachers must access such services in order to practice their profession. Schools must divert resources to disciplinary procedures and juvenile offenses, including possible incarceration, which can scar the future of youthful offenders (Steffgen & Ewen, 2007). Maslow viewed safety as a primary human need, and it is no less so for the adults in a school building than for the youth (McLeod, 2018).

Teachers who had been victimized in school reported feeling re-victimized after the crime as the treatment that they received added insult to injury and crippled their ability to heal (Reddy et al., 2013). Educators reported being treated casually or not taken seriously after the crime, being left alone to deal with confusing forms and reports, being unaccompanied if they were sent from school to the hospital, and essentially treated as though they themselves had committed a crime (Reddy et al., 2013).

Taking a sociological approach to the issue of violence against teachers, Espelage et al. (2013) list a number of factors that can be powerful influences in the fight to end violence to include school demographics, leadership style, teaching methods and styles, school-community relations, parental engagement, and school climate. Espelage et al. (2013) believe that most pre-service teachers aren't necessarily equipped with the skills to manage such conflicts, leaving them vulnerable to attack. With class size increases, and resources diminish, many districts are losing positive gains previously made; thus, threatening the educator's ability to form positive relationships with students and families that would be valuable climate enhancers.

FINAL THOUGHTS

Schools' earliest and most primary purposes were to instill religious beliefs and build character. The vast majority of teaching materials and methods aimed to teach students to read and comprehend religious tomes and learning was done by rote. Students frequently were unmotivated to learn in this manner and discipline was meted out in order to force them into attention. Teaching was not viewed as a profession for several centuries and the most important attribute teachers could have was the physical strength and fortitude to bend students to their will and maintain order in the classroom and schoolyard.

Looking back at the history of violence in American schools, one is struck by the fact that factors associated with such violence have varied greatly in time and place. Some of the variables most often identified as roots of school violence—poverty, intolerance, availability of weapons, overcrowding, or social media—seem clearly related to incidents of school violence during periods in history and locale, yet, they appear to have absolutely no relationship at other times and in other geographies. For these reasons, the questions related to school violence, its causes, and its prevention, are never fully answered.

School violence is not tied to one set of stakeholders in the schools. American history has witnessed violence in many forms to include students against classmates, students against teachers, teachers against students, community against school members, and even adults against adults within a school building. Whether students come to school already predisposed to violent actions, or whether aspects of schooling itself lead to or exacerbate these conditions also is not clear. There are probably as many causes of school violence as there are violent acts themselves.

Given that our nation was birthed from bloody battles, it is not surprising that schools have never been completely absent of conflict, punishment, and violence. As institutions, they mirror the society around them and are plagued by its issues. But with what appears to be escalated violence in contemporary society and social media means to broadcast its effects widely and rapidly, it behooves all school stakeholders to learn from our past so that history does not repeat itself.

POINTS TO REMEMBER

- *School violence is not a new phenomenon in the United States.*
- *There is evidence of violence against students by their teachers that reaches back throughout history and includes physical punishment, isolation, humiliation, and depriving students of certain rights.*
- *The use of corporal punishment in schools as a means of controlling student behavior and motivating disengaged students to learn has been well documented and, according to some authors, may be seen as one of the contributors to create an environment in which violence is accepted as the norm.*
- *Violence against teachers has taken place throughout our country's history and includes incidents of student, parent, community, and staff attacks.*
- *There are a variety of theories attempting to explain school violence, including biological, environmental, and school ecological factors.*
- *While those who act violently are unique as individuals, it appears that they share some commonalities, including failure of empathy, existential rage, suicide and existential angst, failure of manhood, shame and envy, and extreme reactivity.*
- *Violence in schools and school communities also have been the result of perceived injustices in social and educational systems.*

Chapter 2

Actions Around the World

Cross-Cultural Perspectives
on Student Safety

Children have the right to protection from all forms of violence whether it be physical or mental, injury or abuse, neglect or negligent treatment, or sexual abuse (United Nations General Assembly, 2016). Although there are more than one billion children that attend school around the world, many of them do not enjoy their right to a safe and stimulating learning environment (United Educational, Scientific, and Cultural Organization [UNESCO], 2017).

Today, students are exposed to, and victims of, many forms of bullying to include cyberbullying, sexual and gender-based violence, corporal punishment, and other forms of violence such as schoolyard fighting, gang violence, and assault with weapons (UNESCO, 2017). Although rates of youth violence have declined over time, youth violence remains the second leading cause of death for adolescents (Volungis & Goodman, 2017).

School violence and bullying in all forms is a global concern that stems from gender and social norms in addition to wider structural and contextual factors such as income inequality, deprivation, marginalization, and conflict and, thus, warrants global collaboration in preventative efforts. (UNESCO, 2017; UNICEF, 2017). An estimated 246 million children and adolescents experience school violence in some form every year and data from Europe, North America, and Australasia suggest that bullying is the most common form of school violence (Volungis & Goodman, 2017; United National General Assembly, 2016).

School violence and bullying not only violate the rights of children and adolescents to an education, it has a demonstrably negative impact on students' academic performance, physical and mental health, and emotional well-being, particularly those students who are victimized, and creates an atmosphere of anxiety, fear, and insecurity, impacting the entire school community (UNESCO, 2017; Sherr, Hensels, Skeen, Tomlinson, Roberts, & Macedo, 2016).

11

SCOPE OF SCHOOL VIOLENCE

School violence is more than just physical violence; it also includes corporal punishment, psychological violence such as verbal abuse, sexual violence, such as rape and harassment, and bullying and cyberbullying (UNESCO, 2017). School violence and bullying can be perpetrated not only by other students but by teachers, other school staff, and members of the wider community. Violence perpetrated by peers must be differentiated from violence perpetrated by educational institutions and/or their representatives as this difference will significantly shape both the impact of, and the response to, the violence (UNESCO, 2017).

Gender-based violence is prevalent in schools and results in the physical, sexual, or psychological harm or suffering of a student that stems from gender discrimination, gender role expectations, gender stereotypes, or is based on gender-linked differential power status (UNESCO, 2017; UNICEF, 2017). Evidence suggests that girls are more likely to experience sexual violence and boys are more likely to experience corporal punishment in school (UNESCO, 2017).

Children and adolescents who are economically disadvantaged, from migrant or refugee communities, hold linguistic, ethnic, or cultural minority status, and are disabled are the most vulnerable and thus, are at higher risk of school violence and bullying (Maynard, Vaughn, Salas-Wright, & Vaughn, 2016). In addition, those students whose sexual orientation and/or gender identity or expression does not conform to traditional social or gender norms are at risk for school violence (Wyss, 2014).

School violence and bullying can occur inside and outside the classroom, around school property, on the way to or from school, and online. In school, violence and bullying are often invisible, and even ignored, as they occur in places such as bathrooms, locker rooms, hallways, and playgrounds where students are less likely to be seen or supervised by educational staff (Pipe, 2014). In some cultures, corporal punishment, fighting, and bullying are seen as a normal part of discipline and adults are unaware of the negative impact it has on the education, health, and well-being of the students (UNESCO, 2017; Crews & Counts, 1997).

Prevalence and Impact of School Violence

School violence and bullying occurs around the world and affects a significant proportion of the world's students. While the number varies between 10 percent and 65 percent depending on the country and research study, an estimated 246 million children experience school violence and bullying in some form every year (UNESCO, 2017).

Research shows that school violence and bullying harm the physical health and emotional well-being of students and that physical violence, such as corporal punishment, can cause fatal or non-fatal physical harm (Gershoff, 2016). In addition, student victims of bullying are more likely to experience interpersonal difficulties, be depressed, lonely or anxious, have low self-esteem, and have suicidal thoughts or attempt suicide (Langman, 2009).

Violence can also significantly impact a student's education. Students may be afraid to attend school, miss class, avoid school activities, or even drop out of school altogether (UNICEF, 2017). International research demonstrates that bullying reduces students' achievement in key subject areas such as math due to the inability to concentrate, among other emotional effects (UNESCO, 2017; Sherr et al., 2016). Education for all students, not just those who have been victimized, is also reduced due to fear of an unsafe learning environment and the perception that teachers do not care about student well-being and have no control (Randa & Wilcox, 2010).

BULLYING

Available research from Europe, North America, and Australasia suggests that three in ten students have admitted to bullying others, making it the most common form of school violence; however, corporal punishment is common in many other regions of the world (UNESCO, 2017, United Nations General Assembly, 2016; UNICEF, 2017). Three national studies conducted in the United States reported that the most common forms of bullying include verbal insults, name calling, hitting, direct aggression, theft, threats, spreading rumors, and social exclusion or isolation (Bauer, 2017; UNESCO, 2017).

In South Africa and Malawi, research shows that educational outcomes are severely affected by bullying, violence, and "harsh punishment" (Sherr et al., 2016, p. 36). While in India, Peru, and Viet Nam, students reported that indirect and relational types of bullying, such as humiliation and social exclusion, were most common (UNESCO, 2017; UNICEF, 2017). Students from lower castes in India, for example, are more likely to be humiliated and denigrated by higher caste teachers than their higher caste peers (UNESCO, 2017).

An Australian study found that while both boys and girls were equally subjected to teasing, boys were more likely to be physically bullied and threatened while girls were more likely to be deliberately left out (Vassallo, Edwards, Renda, & Olsson, 2014; UNICEF, 2017). It was also found that boys and girls reacted differently to bullying. Although feeling angry about it, boys were less likely to admit being bothered by the victimizing behavior while girls just felt sad and miserable (UNESCO, 2017). Boys from the United States are also more likely to be the victims of physical violence than girls (Shetgiri, 2017).

CYBERBULLYING

In Europe, 80 percent of children between the ages of 5 and 14 have cell phones, placing them at increased risk of cyberbullying and being exposed to hate messages and self-harm sites. From 2010 through 2014, the percentage of children, particularly girls, between the ages of 9 and 16, who had experienced cyberbullying rose from 8 percent to 12 percent (Lindert, 2017; United Nations General Assembly, 2016).

According to the United States' 2013 Youth Risk Behavior Survey, 15 percent of ninth to twelfth grade students were bullied electronically through emails, chat rooms, instant messaging, websites, or texting, with girls being more than twice as likely (21 percent) to report victimization than boys (9 percent) (Gordon, 2014).

LGBTQ+

Violence experienced by LGBTQ+ students is proportionally higher than their non-LGBTQ+ peers and was found to be as little as 16 percent in Nepal and as high as 85 percent in the United States (UNESCO, 2017; McKay, Misra, & Lindquist, 2017). In New Zealand, lesbian, gay, and bisexual students were three times more likely to be bullied than their heterosexual peers and transgender students were five times more likely to be bullied while in Norway, 15 percent to 48 percent of LGBTQ+ students were bullied compared to 7 percent of heterosexual students (UNESCO, 2017). Similarly, Asian studies demonstrate that the proportion of LGBTQ+ students who experience bullying in school ranges from 7 percent in Mongolia to 68 percent in Japan (UNESCO, 2017).

Students who are not LGBTQ+ but are perceived by their peers not to conform to culturally accepted gender norms are also targets of homophobic violence (Wyss, 2014; Payne & Smith, 2013). For example, in Thailand, 24 percent of heterosexual students were the victims of school violence because their gender expression was perceived as non-conforming and, in Canada, 33 percent of male students experienced verbal violence related to their perceived sexual orientation (UNESCO, 2017).

PHYSICAL VIOLENCE AND CORPORAL PUNISHMENT

Physical violence, including corporal punishment, is a significant problem in schools around the world, with peers and teachers being the most common perpetrators (UNESCO, 2017). In a survey of teachers and students from

Swaziland, Namibia, Botswana, and Lesotho, 70 percent to 96 percent of respondents stated that verbal and physical violence occurs in their school with 18 percent to 44 percent of respondents stating that the violence is related to sexual diversity (UNESCO, 2017). Although boys are more likely to report being physically attacked at school than girls, South Africa has found that 6 percent of both boys and girls reported being physically attacked or hurt at school while 22 percent of boys and girls reported being threatened, robbed, or assaulted (Netshitangani, 2014).

Over half of all children across the globe live in countries where corporal punishment is still allowed under law (UNESCO, 2017). It has been reported that 732 million school-age children between the ages of 6 and 17 live in countries where corporal punishment at school is not fully prohibited (UNICEF, 2017). Countries in the Middle East and North Africa have used methods such as caning to punish students for poor academic performance while other countries use corporal punishment to correct misbehavior (UNESCO, 2017).

In South Africa, 8 percent of secondary school girls had experienced severe sexual assault or rape while at school and 6.2 percent of students in Germany and 1.1 percent in Belgium had experienced sexual abuse (UNESCO, 2017; Netshitangani, 2014). Sexual harassment by teachers is also common. Latin American teachers have used sexual coercion and abuse in exchange for better grades while male teachers in Africa coerce girls who cannot afford school-related expenses into sexual relationships (UNESCO, 2017).

Reports indicate that in India, 78 percent of 8-year-old students and 34 percent of 15-year-old students had been physically punished at least once in the past week by teachers at schools (Nijhara, Bhatia, & Unnikrishnan, 2018). Similarly, in Ethiopia, 38 percent of 8-year-old students and 12 percent of 15-year-old students reported physical punishment by teachers at least once in the last week, while 30 percent of 8-year-old students and 7 percent of 15-year-old students in Peru reported punishment at least once per week (UNICEF, 2017, Wonde, Jibat, & Baru, 2014).

A COMPREHENSIVE RESPONSE

The education system as a whole, the surrounding communities, and involved stakeholders, all have a responsibility to protect students from violence and provide a safe and inclusive learning environment for every student (Mushert, Henry, Bracy, & Peguero, 2014). Communities that take a two-pronged approach that includes interventions to both prevent and address school violence and bullying as well as fostering the development and maintenance of trusting relationships to the school environment, have been shown to reduce school violence and bullying (Volungis & Goodman, 2017; Mushert et al., 2014).

A comprehensive response system should involve strong leadership, a safe and inclusive school environment, the development of knowledge, attitudes and skills, effective partnerships, and appropriate reporting mechanisms that provide for support services (Mushert et al., 2014). More specifically, response systems should embody the enactment and enforcement of national laws and policies and school policies and codes of conduct as well as embrace a commitment to creating safe, inclusive, and supportive learning environments for all students (UNESCO, 2017).

Teachers should be trained and supported in positive forms of discipline as well as the delivery of relevant curricula and learning materials (Volungis & Goodman, 2017; Mushert et al., 2014). Equally important, it is vital to have safe, confidential, and student-friendly reporting mechanisms and support services in place to support the culture and climate of the building and to ensure that all stakeholders know there is a way to report behaviors seen as unsafe (Mushert et al., 2014; UNESCO, 2017).

LEADERSHIP, LAW, AND POLICY

Legislation is a key element of a comprehensive response to violence against students and conveys a clear message to society condemning violence against children, sets out guidance on protection measures, and provides redress and a means to fight for children's rights (United Nation General Assembly, 2016). At the district and school levels, leadership teams should develop and enforce staff policies and codes of conduct (Winn, 2018; Mushert et al., 2014).

Laws on School Violence and Bullying

Legislation may involve the establishment of a dedicated body to tackle cyberbullying, including the investigation of complaints, setting standards for online safety, liaising with internet intermediaries and force users to remove content and material (United Nations General Assembly, 2016; Winn, 2018).

Various countries around the world have specific legislation regarding school violence and bullying. For example, the Republic of Korea established an anti-school violence and bullying law for the prevention of and countermeasure against violence in schools (UNESCO, 2017). In order to protect the human rights of students and raise them as healthy members of society, Korea developed a master plan that called for research and education, support and rehabilitation, partnerships between agencies and educational institutions, and placement of school counselors (UNESCO, 2017).

The Philippines Anti-Bullying Act provides a framework for national awareness-raising initiatives and school policies and requires all elementary and secondary schools to adopt policies addressing bullying and establishing relevant reporting mechanisms and requirements with sanctions for non-compliance (Disini Law Office, 2015). In Finland, Section 29 of the Basic Education Act provides every student with the right to a safe school environment and places the responsibility for ensuring that students do not experience violence and bullying at school with education authorities (Malekian & Nordlof, 2012).

Similarly, in Sweden, the 2009 Discrimination Act and 2010 Education Act prohibits any form of discrimination and bullying in schools and, under the Education Act, schools must develop annual plans to prevent and address violence while investigating and reporting all incidents of bullying that do occur (UNESCO, 2015). Reprisals against those that report incidents of bullying are prohibited and damages may be awarded if schools do not comply with the regulations (UNECO, 2015).

The laws in Canada are province specific with Ontario stating that safety rules are effective only in public schools, while in the province of Quebec the responsibility is on school boards as well as public and private schools to maintain a healthy and safe learning environment for its students (UNECO, 2017). Many other countries do not have any specific legislation regarding school violence and bullying but cover the matter by broader, relevant laws, such as anti-discrimination, human rights, and equality laws (UNESCO, 2017). Students in Ireland for example, are protected from bullying by federal law (UNESCO, 2017).

Although the United States has no single anti-bullying law at the federal level, a framework is provided by laws such as The Improving America Schools Act and Safe and Drug-Free Schools and Communities Act (UNESCO, 2017). Bullying is covered under discriminatory, harassment, and federal civil rights laws enforced by the Department of Education and the Department of Justice (UNESCO, 2017). Laws and state education codes have also been enacted at the state level to prevent school bullying and protect children (UNESCO, 2017). Most recently, new legislation has been passed to increase protection in public schools (Winn, 2018).

Laws on Cyberbullying

As with bullying, certain countries have adopted specific legislation concerning cyberbullying or have specifically included cyberbullying in antibullying legislation (UNESCO, 2017). In the United States, California passed a bill that enables schools to suspend students who engage in cyberbullying through social networking sites using mobile phones and other internet services (Prall, 2014).

The United States Department of Education has enacted various policy actions to battle cyberbullying including requiring public schools to report incidents, creating professional development opportunities for school bus drivers and classroom teachers, and leading the Asian American Pacific Islanders Bullying Prevention Taskforce to explore the unique issues faced by this population of students (UNESCO, 2017).

To address distinct aspects of cyberbullying some countries have established specific offenses such as student harassment, disclosure of intimate photographs without consent, and malicious impersonation online (United Nations General Assembly, 2016). New Zealand, for example, has adopted the Harmful Digital Communications Act which criminalizes the sending of messages and the posting of material online that deliberately causes serious emotional distress or incitement to suicide (O'Brien, 2015). This act aims to deter and prevent harmful communications, reduce victim impact, and establish systems for complaint resolution and the removal of damaging online material (O'Brien, 2015).

Similarly, the Australian Enhancing Online Safety for Children Act was created in 2015 and amended in 2017 (Australia, 2017). This act established a Children's eSafety Commissioner to administer a complaint system for cyberbullying material and provides for the quick removal of damaging material posted on social media that targets students while concurrently promoting online safety for all (Australia, 2017).

SCHOOL MANAGEMENT

School governance and management structures have a duty of care to students and must clearly communicate that violence and bullying are unacceptable. Research proves that safe schools are characterized by strong management and effective school leaders (Wang, Berry, & Swearer, 2013; Cohen & Freiberg, 2013).

School policies should identify individual responsibilities and actions to prevent violence and bullying while codes of conduct for teachers should explicitly refer to violence and abuse (Wang, Berry, & Swearer, 2013). Penalties should be clearly stipulated and consistent with applicable legal frameworks for children's rights and protection (Cohen &Freiberg, 2013). For example, in Kenya, teachers found in breach of professional conduct may be disciplined from a range of penalties that include suspension, interdiction, or deregistration (UNESCO, 2017).

CAPACITY

School administrators and teachers must be trained and supported in the knowledge and understanding of school violence and bullying to help the prevention, identification, and response to incidents of violence and bullying among students (Weise, 2014). More specifically, professional development opportunities on school violence should include positive, gender-sensitive, non-violent approaches to discipline and classroom management (Weise, 2014). Teachers should also be trained on how to assist students in building the capacity to recognize, prevent, and respond to violence and bullying through the impartation of essential knowledge, values, and skills (Temkin, 2012).

Research has uncovered a range of initiatives to support teachers in different countries (UNESCO, 2017). The country of Jordan, for example, has over 4,000 school teachers and counselors that have been trained in classroom management skills and positive discipline (UNESCO, 2017). Argentina and Chile have both created workshops for students and parents as well as clinical care for victims and bullies to prevent future incidents (UNESCO, 2017).

Under its Anti-Bullying Manifesto, Norway's creation of the Zero program has resulted in its implementation in over 400 schools (UNESCO, 2017). This program provides guidance for school staff on how to identify, prevent, and resolve bullying by integrating anti-bullying efforts within general schoolwork (UNESCO, 2017).

Hong Kong's youth development program, Project PATHS, assists students in developing the life skills necessary to become proactive, helpful bystanders when they observe any form of bullying (UNESCO, 2017). The program includes general awareness-raising on bullying, time for self-reflection, and opportunities for students to practice any newly learned behavior (UNESCO, 2017).

PARTNERSHIPS

Many adults are unaware of the extent of school violence and its negative impact on the well-being of their students. Raising awareness with the school and parental community, as well as within the students themselves, is essential in building partnerships to tackle school violence and bullying (UNESCO, 2017). Students should be viewed as equal partners in the fight to prevent bullying and should be included in planning and implementing programs to reduce school violence (UNESCO, 2017).

Various countries have found unique ways to raise awareness regarding the issues surrounding bullying and violence. Canada declared a National Pink Shirt Day while Mexico focused awareness efforts at the local level by providing parents with information, support, and assistance to identify and address changes in student behavior linked to cyberbullying (UNESCO, 2017).

The United States has formed various campaigns such as Take a Stand: Stop Bullying Now and National Bullying Prevention Awareness Month, to raise public awareness as well as a comprehensive website that provides information on the nature of bullying/cyberbullying, who is considered at risk, and how bullying can be prevented and addressed (US Department of Health and Human Services, n.d.). The site also includes suggestions for parents and students about how, when, and where to report cases of cyberbullying (US Department of Health and Human Services, n.d.).

Comprehensive responses to school violence and bullying must also involve partnerships between the education sector and the wider community, including the media, parents, and families. Working with parents and communities is critical in reducing the incidents of violence and bullying on the way to and from school as well as in reinforcing the promotion of nonviolence in schools (US Department of Health and Human Services, n.d.).

The Anti-Bullying Manifesto in Norway, while only lasting two years, not only identified local authoritative measures such as anti-bullying interventions in schools, but also had the distinction of finding key stakeholders in preventing bullying, including the national government, local and regional authorities, trade unions, education unions, and the national parents' committee, and emphasized cooperation and collaboration as measures to ensure that legal provisions surrounding school violence and safety were implemented (eNCA, 2016).

East Africa's Action Aid's Stop Violence Against Girls project highlights the importance of partnerships with communities and the value of working together with established local women's groups and child rights organizations (Parkes & Heslop, 2011). Research into the project found that these relationships were important for discussion of sensitive issues, such as corporal punishment (Parkes & Heslop, 2011). In addition, involving traditional and religious leaders was found to be an effective strategy to secure buy-in and support for addressing school violence and addressing disparities among gender (Parkes & Heslop, 2011).

In Afghanistan, the Children's Violence Free Schools project emphasizes the involvement of children and their meaningful participation in school structures. Their focus is on the development and implementation of school-based child protection systems that protect children from school violence and abuse and involve the establishment of three different committees in each school (Wood, 2011). The child protection committee was created to address specific issues found in school while the parent, teacher, and student association helps facilitate dialogue between the community and the outside community. The student council was formed to promote communication between students and assist them in self-organization and how to address the issues that affect them (Wood, 2011).

In 2015, the #PurpleMySchool campaign was launched by UNESCO, UNDP, and Being LGBTQ+ in Asia, with the goal of ensuring that all educational settings are free from bullying and discrimination based on sexual orientation and gender identity or expression (BLIA, 2015). As part of the campaign, peers, teachers, parents, secondary educational schools, and universities were encouraged to become allies of LGBTQ+ students and wear, draw, or make something in purple that could be promoted on the campaign website (BLIA, 2015).

SERVICES AND SUPPORT

It is critical that victims of bullying and bystanders are afforded effective, accessible, confidential, age and gender-sensitive reporting mechanisms that do not put them at further risk (UNESCO, 2017). Some schools have implemented telephone helplines, chatrooms and online reporting, and clubs that have been created as safe spaces to raise concerns about and report sexual violence (UNESCO, 2017).

Plan Kenya and Childline Kenya have set up a free 24-hour telephone helpline for children that provides both preventive and support services through referral and school outreach facilities (Li, 2013). Similarly, the Netherlands, formed an anonymous helpline for children under the age of 18 to discuss a range of concerns, including bullying at school either via phone or a 30-minute online conversation. Research demonstrated that students who sought help via both methods experienced a higher sense of well-being and a reduced severity of their problems (Fukkink, Bruns, & Ligvoet, 2016).

In addition to safe reporting mechanisms, victims, perpetrators, and bystanders of school violence should be afforded the benefit of safe, easily accessible, child-sensitive, confidential and independent counseling and support (Gordon, 2018). Professional development is an essential component of all programs as educators serve as the first point of contact and can provide guidance and advice as well as employing school counselors or social workers that can deal directly with the students involved in incidents of violence (Gordon, 2018).

School counselors can have a significant impact on preventing school violence by modeling and training teachers in the basic counseling skills that they can then use in their everyday interactions with students (Volungis & Goodman, 2017. This consistent application of counseling relationships and communication skills in everyday, micro-level interactions with students will create and foster a learning environment that is filled with trusting relationships that promote school violence prevention (Volungis & Goodman, 2017).

Through a pilot of the Collaborative and Proactive Solutions program, the United States was able to place counselors in schools to work closely with the most disruptive and aggressive students to help them develop strategies to address their needs and change their behavior as an alternative to traditional punishment methods (Greene, 2015). The pilot demonstrated an 80 percent reduction in suspensions, disciplinary referrals, and incidents of peer aggression (Greene, 2015).

Countries such as Ghana and Malawi use trained and trusted community volunteers to work as counselors for the USAID Safe Schools program, which focuses on gender-based violence in schools (Centre for Educational Research and Training and DevTech Systems, Inc., 2008). Volunteers included village leaders, school staff, individuals from parent-teacher associations, and community committees who were trained in basic listening skills, children's rights and responsibilities and methods to prevent, respond to, and report incidents of violence (Centre for Educational Research and Training and DevTech Systems, Inc., 2008). As a result of the program, students reported that the counseling services had helped them deal with being a victim of violence as well as work through conflict and anger management issues (Centre for Educational Research and Training and DevTech Systems, Inc., 2008).

In Japan, peer support and counseling has been found effective in dealing with the social exclusion of students (UNESCO, 2017). Various forms of peer support have been used and include the training of older students to help younger students and the formation of anonymous support methods such as the anonymous submittal of problems into a box that are then read by peer supporters who provide possible solutions via a handout or written newsletter that is available to all students (UNESCO, 2017).

CHALLENGES TO A COMPREHENSIVE RESPONSE

Despite all the various initiatives around the world to address school violence and bullying, there are very few countries actually taking a comprehensive approach. Challenges include the lack of legislation and policies or the weak enforcement of any existing legislation and policies to protect students from school violence (Richardson, 2107). This may, in part, be due to the lack of awareness among education policy makers, planners, and professionals of the harmful effects of school violence and bullying on the education, health, and well-being of students (Espelage, n.d.).

There is also a limited capacity for the resources necessary to train and support teachers and other school staff in the prevention of school violence and bullying, identification and responsiveness to incidents of violence, and the use of nonviolent approaches to classroom management and discipline (UNESCO, 2017).

The under-reporting of school violence and bullying leads to limited data on the causes, nature, scale, and impact of school violence and is particularly problematic in that students lack safe, accessible, confidential, and child-friendly reporting mechanisms (UNESCO, 2017). Student involvement in planning and implementing interventions to prevent school violence and make schools safer has thus far been limited and would need to increase if a comprehensive response to school violence is to be implemented (Espelage, n.d.).

COMPREHENSIVE RESPONSE PROGRAMS

There have been significant measures at the national level to prevent and address school violence and bullying such as public awareness campaigns, efforts to inform and assist children, the enactment of public policies and legislation, early detection and response efforts, and restorative practices to repair harm and relationships while avoiding recidivism (United Nations General Assembly, 2016).

More specifically, anti-bullying initiatives include the strengthening of values, concern for others, and students' sense of responsibility in preventing discrimination through ethical communication (United Nations General Assembly, 2016). Focus is given to how students can protect themselves, cope with the emotional result of victimization, enhance resilience, make good decisions, strengthen positive value and life skills, and take responsibility for their actions toward others (United Nations General Assembly, 2016).

Olweus Bullying Prevention Program

In Norway, the Olweus Bullying Prevention Program is a model approach for reducing and preventing bullying that has been implemented in other countries including Canada, Croatia, England, Germany, Iceland, Sweden, and the United States (Hazelden Foundation, 2016). The program works at the school, classroom, and individual levels and provides methods to involve and secure the support of parents and the community. It highlights the responsibility of adults to ensure children's participation in decisions, to impart the skills necessary to prevent bullying, and to act as good role models (Hazelden Foundation, 2016).

Although school administrators and teachers are primarily responsible for program implementation, the participation of all students is essential, with victims and perpetrators both receiving individualized interventions (Hazelden Foundation, 2016). Research has demonstrated the effectiveness of the Olweus program in promoting a safer and more positive school environment, including improved social climates, and the reduction of bullying and related anti-social behaviors (Hazelden Foundation, 2016).

Safe and Enabling School Environment Program

Croatia's Safe and Enabling School Environment program was implemented to protect children from school violence and bullying and consists of two parts. The first part includes a public "Stop Violence among Children" campaign that raises awareness of aggression and bullying and promotes social change (Zgance et al., 2012). The second part is comprised of school-based interventions that prevent and address school violence and help schools remain safe, including the involvement of students in school policy decisions and actions to reduce violence (Zgance et al., 2012).

Evaluations of the program have shown a reduction in the incidence of frequent bullying from 10 percent to 5 percent and a reduction in the number of students bullying others from 13 percent to 3 percent (Zgance et al., 2012). Under the program, teachers reported being better able to recognize bullying and felt more prepared to stop it, while 80 percent of students knew who to turn to for help (Zgance et al., 2012). As a result, similar programs have subsequently been launched in Serbia, Bulgaria, Montenegro, Slovenia, and Kazakhstan (Zgance et al., 2012).

Safe Schools Program

USAID's Safe Schools Program model aims to reduce gender-based violence in and around schools through an integrated set of interventions at the national, institutional, local, and individual levels (Centre for Educational Research and training and DevTech Systems, Inc., 2008). Interventions include national awareness-raising activities with a range of stakeholders, teacher training to recognize, prevent, and respond to gender-based violence, and community awareness-raising (Centre for Educational Research and training and DevTech Systems, Inc., 2008). The implementation of this program has resulted in changes in teachers' attitudes toward the acceptability of corporal punishment, an increase in teachers' awareness of sexual harassment, and an increase in students' awareness of their right not to be hurt or mistreated (Centre for Educational Research and training and DevTech Systems, Inc., 2008).

Learn without Fear Campaign

Plan International's Learn without Fear campaign is a global effort in more than forty-four countries to end violence against children in schools and addresses a range of violence issues, including sexual abuse, neglect, verbal, and emotional abuse, corporal punishment, bullying, peer-to-peer violence, youth gangs, harassment, and the use of weapons in and around schools (Plan International, 2008).

The campaign has contributed to changes in legislation, the creation of safer schools and communities, and increased awareness of violence in schools with anti-violence campaign messages reaching over 94 million adults and children through radio and television shows, leaflets, training sessions, and workshops (Plan International, 2008). Students are critically involved in all aspects of the campaign, ranging from campaign planning in Malawi and Egypt to running radio shows in Senegal and participating in regional art collaborations in Asia (Plan International, 2008).

As a result of this campaign, more than 19,000 teachers have been trained in nonviolent teaching methods and more than thirty-three countries have reported an increase in nonviolent practices among educators (UNESCO, 2017). In more than twenty-seven countries, improvements have been made in student reporting mechanisms and more than thirty-six countries provide access to medical support for school violence–reported injuries (UNESCO, 2017).

KiVa

Finland's KiVa anti-bullying program focuses on prevention, consideration of individual cases, and monitoring changes over time and is used in 90 percent of comprehensive schools throughout the country (Andone, 2017). Teachers are encouraged to invest in the importance of listening to students and ensuring that they have a voice. Program recommendations to help teachers address bullying immediately, as it occurs in the classroom, include mandatory pre-service teacher training and all-staff trainings on bullying prevention and cessation (Andone, 2017). As a result of KiVa's implementation, national rates of bullying and victimization have decreased (Andone, 2017).

SCHOOL CONNECTEDNESS

Treating students with dignity and respect is a key component of school connectedness and is often associated with the successful prevention and resolution of violent school events (Volungis & Goodman, 2017; American Psychological Association [APA], 2018). Attachments to school personnel and the extent to which students feel connected to their school community and environment can influence how they respond to perceived injustices. Students who feel connected engage in fewer disruptive and oppositional type behaviors, experience more stable social-emotional well-being, and have higher academic achievement than students who feel less connected (Volungis & Goodman, 2017; Benbenishty, Astor, Rozier, & Wrabel, 2016).

Students are also less likely to commit acts of violence when they can trust, feel close to, and look up to their teachers and feel that their own thoughts and feelings are validated (Benbenishty et al., 2016). Feelings of alienation, being a victim of school bullying, and the lack of a positive role model to emulate effective problem-solving strategies are significant risk factors for school violence (Volungis & Goodman, 2017).

Oftentimes, perpetrators of school violence share their plans with other students before the violent act takes place (Benbenishty et al., 2016). As a result of school-connectedness and strong student-teacher relationships, students are more willing to speak up when they have knowledge about a potential act of school violence and perpetrators may be more willing to seek help before actually committing a violent act (Volungis & Goodman, 2017).

RESTORATIVE APPROACHES

The goal of restorative practices is to repair harm and mend relationships rather than doling out punishment and retribution. Restorative practices in an educational setting serve as an alternative to traditional disciplinary measures such as suspension or expulsion and help reintegrate perpetrators of violence into the school community (Watchel, 2016). In addition, schools can conduct victim-offender mediation, group conferences that include training on conflict resolution, and the training of student mediators to help resolve conflicts among their peers (Watchel, 2016).

Restorative approaches give students the chance to tell things from their perspective, be listened to, resolve negative feelings, and establish a sense of restitution (Fronius, Persson, Guckenburg, Hurley, & Petrosino, 2016). Through this approach, students who have engaged in bullying behavior can begin to understand and take responsibility for any harm caused, and to actively engage in solutions to provide restitution and prevent recidivism (Ortega, Lyubansky, Nettles, & Espelage, 2016).

Evidence from several new research studies suggests that restorative practices may have positive effects that include improvement in school attendance, climate and culture, an increase in community and parent engagement, a decrease in the use of exclusionary discipline, increased student connectedness, and decreased levels of bullying (Fronius et al., 2016; Ortega et al., 2016).

Student participation and contribution needs to be at the forefront of restorative efforts; they must be empowered and must be provided the skills and confidence to stand up against bullying and seek help in strengthening a positive peer culture and becoming effective agents in preventing school violence (Watchel, 2016). Equally as important, students should be involved in developing initiatives to prevent bullying and create violence-free schools (Ortega et al., 2016).

FINAL THOUGHTS

School violence is a global concern that effects millions of students in some form every year and can significantly impact a student's education. Violence, even in times of peace, often prevents students from attending school, classes, activities, and can even result in students dropping out of school altogether. For those students that do stay in school and attend, unsafe learning environments can result in lower academic achievement and success, particularly in the subject areas of math, due to the inability to concentrate and other emotional effects.

Students are vulnerable to all forms of violence at all times. There is a recent, growing trend of violent attacks and school shootings, particularly in the United States, that have significantly affected the health and well-being of not only students, teachers, administrators, and their school community, but parents, adults, other children, and communities worldwide.

To combat school violence, it is essential to remember that everyone has a responsibility to protect all students from violence as well as to provide a safe and inclusive learning environment. Comprehensive approaches to school violence should be utilized across the school environment and include interventions that both prevent and address violence in school as well as foster the development and maintenance of trusting relationships within the school environment.

In any approach to the prevention of school violence, students should be treated with respect and as equal partners in the fight. They should be included in the planning and implementation of violence-reduction programs within their school as well as in any policy making and decisions. Students should also be taught and counseled on how they can protect themselves against violence, cope with the resultant emotions of being victimized, build and enhance resistance, and most importantly, take responsibility for their actions toward others.

Through the use of restorative practices, students can find their voice to express thoughts and feelings from their perspective, be genuinely listened to, feel connected to their school and teachers, and be given the opportunity to repair any harm done and mend relationships. School violence will not end until students are able to take full responsibility for their own behavior and actively engage in the solutions needed to end school violence.

POINTS TO REMEMBER

- *All children have the right to protection from all forms of violence including those children who are economically disadvantaged, hold a minority status, and/or are disabled.*
- *School violence violates the rights of students to an education and has a discernibly negative impact on students' academic performance, physical health, and mental and emotional well-being.*
- *Over half of all children around the world reside and go to school in countries where corporal punishment is still allowed under law and widely used to punish students for poor academic performance and to correct misbehavior.*
- *School administrators and teachers should be afforded professional development opportunities that will aid in the prevention, identification, and response to school violence. These trainings should include positive, gender-sensitive, non-violent approaches to discipline and classroom management as well as any necessary knowledge and/or skills that will allow teachers to recognize, prevent, and respond to violence.*
- *Perpetrators share their plans with other students before committing the violent act itself; thus, strong student-centered relationships should be developed and maintained to allow students a comfortable and trustworthy outlet for revealing any knowledge of potential violent acts or a space for potential perpetrators to seek help before committing any acts of violence.*
- *Students should also be empowered to stand up against bullying, strengthen positive school cultures, and develop anti-bullying initiatives and efforts.*
- *Restorative practices have positive effects and can improve school attendance, improve school climate and culture, increase student connectedness, increase community and parent engagement, decrease the use of discipline, and decrease levels of bullying.*

Chapter 3

Bad Behavior in School and Cyberspace

Bullying and Its Role in School Violence

In an extensive investigation into case studies of school shooters during the period of 1979–2009, Klein (2012) noted incredible similarities among the cases. Perpetrators almost consistently expressed displeasure in perceived injustices that called their masculinity into question; either being rejected by a girl or others (Horton, 2018). This was even true in situations where "the shooters lashed out against their schools for perceived injustices related to discipline or academic assessments" (Klein, 2012, p. 1).

Rather than looking solely to external factors such as severe mental illness, easy access to weapons, or media violence for answers to school violence, considerations must also include questions about what elements of schools themselves cause so many students to suffer from anxiety, depression, fear, rage, or general unhappiness (Klein, 2012; Horton, 2017). There are inextricable relationships among school violence, everyday bullying, and "destructive gender pressures and social demands" (Klein, 2012, p. 3). Despite zero-tolerance policies and other interventions adopted by schools, the quieter forms of violence of everyday school interactions remain, and perhaps have even escalated.

Through qualitative interviews with students that are diverse in geographic location, ethnicity, and social class, Klein (2012) delved into their perceptions about the culture of schools and the common experiences that students had gone through. Key traits of everyday school culture that relate to bullying and school violence in a variety of forms were found.

THREE ELEMENTS OF THE BULLY SOCIETY

Klein (2012) identified three key traits of the bully society in schools (and elsewhere). The first trait is gender policing, which involves conformity to gender expectations (Klein, 2012). Both students and many adults in our schools keep constant vigil to make certain that students conform to what they believe to be specific "boy" and "girl" behavioral codes (Klein, 2012). School community members, then, take on the role of gender police and must become hypersensitive to both their own and others' expressions of what is appropriate and acceptable and is shown through one's attitude, behavior, dress, and values (Klein, 2012).

The second element is masculinity imperatives, and this references the dominant gender norm espoused and enforced by the gender police—that of hypermasculinity (Klein, 2012). Predominantly boys, but more recently girls as well, gain their status by acts of aggression and through their willingness to demonstrate how powerful they are at others' expense (Klein, 2012; Horton, 2018).

The third element is normalized bullying, characterized by the use of coercive or violent power to get and keep social status power (Klein, 2012). Students elevate their status through the bullying of those that they perceive are not maintaining social norms, do not have status, or are weaker than they (Klein, 2012). These elements are not developed in a vacuum but come from societal values that Klein (2012) called the bully economy. In societies with extreme income disparities, which cause disparities in other aspects of social life, bullying has become normalized because it is pervasively reflected in contemporary popular media (Klein, 2012).

Cohn and Canter (2003) feel that there is no one explanation for why children and adolescents become bullies, but that three major factors play a role. The first cluster, cites peer group factors as integral to the adoption of a bullying culture; when one must fit in by being aggressive, there is a greater likelihood that anti-social behaviors will flourish.

The second is the cluster of family factors including the amount of adult supervision that children received, the consequences of acts of aggression, the observation of violence within the family or extended family, and the message that they receive about the appropriateness of any forms of aggression or violence (Cohn & Canter, 2003). Their self-concept and expectation about whether the world is a welcoming or hostile place also plays a part.

The third cluster of factors relates to school itself. In schools in which there was little administrative response to bullying, children received tacit reinforcement for their bullying behaviors. Equally as distressing, in schools in which there was little personalization and no positive school culture that intentionally stressed pro-social behaviors, there was more likely to be bullying.

THE EVOLUTION OF CONCERN OVER SCHOOL BULLYING

While there is no doubt that bullies have existed throughout history, the interest in understanding the phenomenon better and creating violence-free schools began in the late 1900s. Traditional definitions of school violence, according to Batsche and Knoff (1994), included assault, theft, and vandalism but did not consider the issue of bullying. As the nation moved toward the year 2000, where the goal was to have drug and violence-free schools, it necessarily widened the scope of what was considered violence against children and adults alike.

In later evolutions of an understanding of what constituted bullying, the notion of individuals feeling fear or intimidation was added to the definition. The term's meaning was then codified by defining it as "a form of aggression in which one or more students physically and/or psychologically (and more recently, sexually) harass another student repeatedly over a period of time. Typically, the action is unprovoked, and the bully is perceived as stronger than the victim" (Batsche & Knoff, 1994, p. 165).

Japan, England, and the Scandanavian countries contributed the bulk of our knowledge about the incidents and effects of bullying prior to the turn of this century. American studies that were conducted found that roughly 75 percent of students answered "yes" to questions about whether they ever had experienced bullying (Smith & Brain, 2000). When the more stringent definition of bullying is used, that number drops off dramatically, leaving between 15–20 percent of school students who will experience some form of bullying in their school years (Johnston et al., 1993). That definition suggests that bullying is something that happens continually over time (Smith & Brain, 2000).

It appears that a typology of bullies has been developed over the years. Floyd (1985) and Greenbaum (1988) found that bullying is intergenerational and that school bullies are victims in their own homes. They emerge from families in which parents share common traits such as being authoritarian; using physical means of punishment; having limited problem-solving skills; are often rejecting; teaching their children to fight back if provoked; and are inconsistent in their parenting style. Olewus (1991), one of the foremost experts on bullying, wrote that bullying is completely about control. Bullies generally are impulsive, have a strong need to dominate other people, and rarely have empathy for their victims (Olweus, 1991). When controlling others through their actions, bullies feel more secure, but that security comes at the expense of their victims (Olweus, 1991).

Olewus (1991) also discovered that bullies were confident of achieving their goals through aggression as their actions were reinforced through goal attainment (positive reinforcement) and removal of a perceived threat. Following bullies longitudinally, about 60 percent of those boys who had bullied in grades six through nine had been convicted of a crime at least once by the time they were 24 years old and 35–40 percent had three or more convictions (Olweus, 1991).

Olewus (1978) also explored the typology of bullies' victims and described two major types—either passive victims or provocative victims. Passive victims were those students who were anxious, did not act in any manner to spur the attack, and were not likely to defend themselves (Olweus, 1978). Passive victims were often lonely at school, without many friends, and exceptionally close to their parents, especially their mothers; they also tended to be smaller and physically less-developed than age mates (Olweus, 1978). On the other hand, provocative victims were hot-headed, anxious, and ready to retaliate if attacked (Olweus, 1978).

Perry and his colleagues (1988) discovered that some of the most extreme victims in their studies were also the most aggressive and, therefore, described bullies as a heterogeneous group and labeled different categories. Their victimized/rejected student corresponded to the aforementioned passive victim, while the victimized/aggressive/rejected student fit the provocative victim profile (Perry, Kusel, & Perry, 1988). Such a student was likely to be bullied by more aggressive children and then turn his frustrations into acts of bullying those he perceived to be weaker.

Perry et al. (1988) described clear implications for school officials and mental health counselors as it became apparent that addressing bullying effectively depended upon understanding the type of bully to be dealt with. It is important to note that the assessment of bullies must take place on an individual basis and the recommendations for treatment or interventions rely on accurate knowledge of the motivations and temperaments of the students themselves (Perry et al., 1988). One clear finding that cuts across studies is that while not all bullies are rejected by their peers, those who suffer from the most serious problems, will also present with potential life-long issues if left untreated.

Early studies tended to find that boys were far more likely to be bullies and to be bullied, and to inflict physical assaults far more often than girls (Perry et al., 1988; Olweus, 1978; Smith & Brain, 2000). Boys were far more apt to use what Olewus (1978) called direct bullying; however, bullying by girls was found to happen as frequently as boys but in a completely different manner. Girl bullying tends to be indirect, employing isolation and social exclusion; thus, it is far subtler and more difficult to observe. It is often referred to as relational aggression, which, according to the Ophelia Project (2012), falls into the category of bullying as well. These subtle acts of aggression may take the form of gossiping or spreading rumors which can be equally hurtful and have similar negative effects on victims but are less overt (Ophelia Project, 2012).

Younger students experience more bullying than older ones, and the bullies are generally older than their victims (Petrosino, Guckenburg, DeVoe, & Hanson, 2010). Once students reach secondary school, they are bullied by age mates. The most pervasive variable affecting whether a child is bullied or not is physical size and strengths. This factor outweighs myriad others, including social class, ethnicity, dress, accent, or weight (Batsche & Knoff, 1994; Petrosino et al., 2010).

CONTEMPORARY DEFINITIONS OF BULLYING

The definition of bullying has gone through several iterations commensurate with the decades in which research was completed. The most recent definition was created and released in 2014 by research leaders in the field of bullying in collaboration with the Department of Education, the Health Resources, and Services Administration (HRSA), and the Centers for Disease Control and Prevention (CDC) (Gladden, Vivolo-Kantor, Hamburger, & Lumpkin, 2014). This new definition is a tool to help gather information as well as a starting point for discussions and states

Bullying is any unwanted aggressive behavior(s) by another youth or group of youths who are not siblings or current dating partners that involves an observed or perceived power imbalance and is repeated multiple times or is highly likely to be repeated. Bullying may inflict harm or distress on the targeted youth including physical, psychological, social, or educational harm. (Gladden et al., 2014, p. 7)

While bullying can lead to violence, it usually is not categorized with more serious forms of school violence involving weapons or vandalism; yet, it is an unacceptable, anti-social, learned behavior that is influenced by such environmental factors as home, school, peer groups, and even the media. Bullies lack a basic respect for the rights of others and are more likely than other children to resort to aggressive or violent acts to solve problems and they worry less about the consequences of taking such actions (Gladden et al., 2014). They are more prone to fighting than their peers and may escalate feelings of frustration into acts of vengeful violence (Swearer & Hymel, 2015).

Swearer and Hymel (2015) concur that bullying behavior can be influenced by myriad factors including an individual's personality traits, relationships within the family, school, or community setting, as well as sources of media and technology such as movies, television, video games, and social media outlets. Bullying is complex and multifaceted, with individuals even taking different roles such as being a bully, being the victim, being a bully victim, or acting as a bystander to bullying (Gladden et al., 2014; Swearer & Hymel, 2015).

The American Academy of Child and Adolescent Psychiatry (2014) recognized that bullying exposed the victim to an array of physical, verbal, or relational means of aggression. More than one in five students reported being bullied; that number translates into approximately 20.8 percent of students in 2016 (PACER Center, 2018). Bullying tends to increase throughout elementary school, peaks in middle school, and declines in high school, and 43 percent of those bullied reported it (PACER Center, 2018). Of incidents that occurred in view of bystanders, 57 percent stopped when someone intervened (PACER Center, 2018).

Cohn and Canter (2003) shed light on why some children and adolescents are more prone to becoming the victims of bullies. Victims appear to send signals to their peers that they are insecure and are likely to avoid retaliation if they are attacked, and they are more likely to be passive, appear physically or emotionally weak, complain, or seek attention from peers (Cohn & Canter, 2003). They more often come from families in which parents act in overprotective ways, so they have developed less effective skills for coping with the behaviors of others (Cohn & Canter, 2003).

CYBERBULLYING

A contemporary twist on school bullying is cyberbullying, which, in many ways, has the potential for even more pernicious effects than that which occurs face-to-face. Every type of bullying that occurs in real time (status wars, gay bashing, slut shaming, and the likes) takes place in cyberspace; however, the difference is that it occurs around the clock, out of the view of officials such as school personnel, and behind anonymous identities (Klein, 2012). Students who fear they may get in trouble with face-to-face bullying in school know that they have the opportunity to strike online. According to PACER Center (2018), 15.5 percent of high school students and 24 percent of middle school students have been cyberbullied, while 20.2 percent of high school students and 45 percent of middle school students have been bullied on in the school campus.

The two most common forms of online bullying were flaming and outing; through flaming, bullies share provocative or abusive posts, while outing involves the sharing of someone's personal information (Klein, 2012). These actions can run the gamut of forwarding personal information or photos, spreading rumors, making threats, or putting a person's private information in places, such as sexual service sites, which endangers the victim. Another form of harassment, common among girls, is to block an individual from being part of groups or chat rooms and this parallels the social isolation that can go on in school (Klein, 2012).

"Sexting," or the sharing of compromising material of a sexual nature, causes further problems, as it can seriously affect both personal privacy and reputation (Madigan & Temple, 2018). This is particularly powerful in girl culture, where one's reputation is an important commodity. Boys may be victims, as well, particularly since this kind of exchange can be manipulated to become the electronic version of gay bashing (Madigan & Temple, 2018). Doctored pictures and other images can appear real and convincing. What youth do not understand is that these pictures and exchanges can become a permanent part of one's record that can be found by colleges or prospective employers with a simple web search (Madigan & Temple, 2018).

Online bullying poses particular problems for schools confronting the bully culture as they are faced with difficult questions about how to deal with online behavior that falls outside of school hours (Hoffman, 2010). A minority of schools have guidelines specific to this kind of bullying, and this is true of local districts as well, leaving the question of whose responsibility this behavior is an unanswered question (Hoffman, 2010). Hoffman (2010) relates the story of a small middle school in New Jersey in which the principal sent an email message to all his parents, saying that "there is absolutely NO reason for any middle school student to be part of a social networking site" and urged anyone bullied or attacked to "IMMEDIATELY GO TO THE POLICE!" (p. 4). He was besieged by angry and obscene texts from parents in the community.

In another vignette, a guidance counselor described the dramas erupting from online exchanges and the particularly devastating effects that cyberbullying has on middle school students (Hoffman, 2010). Particularly disturbing is the fact that middle school students, already at a vulnerable age, are subjected to online voting in which they decide if "a student is fat or stupid or gay, the impact can be devastating" (Hoffman, 2010, p. 4). Hoffman (2010) also describes how using phones for texting rather than talking deprives students of cues such as tone of voice that could help them decipher the intent of online messages more accurately.

BULLYING AGAINST AND AMONG GIRLS

According to Klein's research (2012), boys under the age of 18 are the perpetrator of approximately 25 percent of reported rapes, 50 percent of known child sexual abuse incidents, and they are the most common of school shooters. Shooters commonly have experienced rejection by females and frequently target those who have rejected them (Klein, 2012). These figures are set against a backdrop of acts of sexual harassment and dating violence that are all too common in contemporary American society. One national study of students in eighth to eleventh grades *documents the wide range of harassing behaviors students experienced, from sexual comments, jokes and gestures, to sexual rumors and graffiti, to flashing and mooning, to touching, grabbing and pinching. Some students reported having their clothing pulled off, being physically blocked or cornered, and being forced to kiss or perform other sexual acts.* (Klein, 2012, p. 58)

Even more disconcerting is that adults in many American schools simply do not see these actions or may flat out ignore them seeing those "less extreme behaviors as 'normal,' [and then] may obscure many of the warning signs leading to serious crimes" (Klein, 2012, p. 58). In the cases of extreme violence, such as school shootings, earlier actions were sloughed off as normal boy behavior and went dismissed as possible red flags to subsequent behavior; however, in at least twenty-three of the school shootings (as of 2012), the motives expressed by the perpetrators included rejection, jealousy, frustration or perceived frustration with girls, or the necessity to protect a girlfriend (Klein, 2012).

When violent perpetrators in this age range did live to share their motives, they spoke of specific actions as a means to putting an end to being tormented, to prove their manhood, or to make others fear them. The perpetrators also appeared to be acting out in response to being rejected and/or having word spread about their being rejected; image, it seems, was as important as the act of being dumped by one's paramour. Klein (2012) remarks on the socialization of boys as a major culprit in acts of violence:

Some boys experience rejection by girls as an unbearable reversal of traditional roles. If the rejected male does not have access to alternative coping strategies, or rather, alternative masculinities, he may use violence and aggression to defend his manhood. (p. 61)

Boys who have little success with girls, those who prefer female friendships, or those who are "too nice" to girls are rarely in the top social status at school, and if their behavior is seen to be too far astray from gender norms, they may slide into the dangerous territory of being seen as "gay" (Dastagir, 2017). Boys perceive that they need to have the upper hand in sexual interactions, and rejection of their advances can damage their sense of masculinity and lower their social status (Dastagir, 2017).

Obviously, not all rejections result in extreme emotions or behaviors. As Newman (2004) wrote,

There is, of course, a difference between feeling rejected and feeling emasculated after such rejection. Not all boys who are rejected by girls feel emasculated by the slight. Emasculation happens when a girl is seen in the boy's eyes primarily as a way of demonstrating his masculinity-so young men for whom masculinity has high salience in their self-conception are likely to be particularly wounded by female rejection. (p. 375)

Supporting these statements, nearly 50 percent of students experienced some kind of sexual harassment while in school; yet, girls were more likely to be on the receiving end of harassment and girls were also more likely to be subjected to a physical form of sexual harassment (Hill & Kearl, 2011). One of Klein's (2012) informants described the school culture as a place where the boys would grab the girls' derrieres, try to kiss or hug them, or verbally abuse them and the girls became upset, yet no action was taken.

Verbal abuse against female students (perpetrated both by males and females) hovered around calling individuals "bitches" or "sluts" or "whores." The Hill and Kearl (2011) study confirmed that both boys and girls reported verbal abuse at a rate of 18 percent in equal proportions. Students in Klein's (2012) studies consistently mentioned that while parents might be informed of these incidents or notes would be sent home, no concrete actions were taken, and the behaviors were so normalized that many students seemed unaware that anything was wrong with their actions. It was often implied that girls were "asking for it" by wearing inappropriate clothing.

MEAN GIRLS AND ODD GIRLS OUT

While most of the violent offenders in school shootings, stabbings, and assaults are male, there is a hidden culture of aggression that exists among female students, leading to fierce bullying of different proportions. Simmons (2011) suggested that American culture socializes girls to be caretakers, that is, those who "tend and befriend," and who are the perfect mothers and put others before themselves. As a result of such socialization, girls are valued by their relationships with others. "In my conversations with girls," Simmons (2011) wrote, "many expressed fear that everyday acts of conflict would result in the loss of the people they most cared about . . . Isolation, they cautioned, was irreversible, and so too great a price to be paid" (p. 69).

The history of studying bullying, according to Simmons (2011), has relied on a definition of bullying as direct acts of aggression (physical or verbal) that are levied against targets in environments in which indirect acts of aggression could not even be measured. To study the social lives of girls, however, researchers must employ different definitions and operate in different environments in order to understand female bullying (Simmons, 2011; Centifanti, Fanti, Thomson, Demetriou, & Anastassiou-Hadjicharalambous, 2015). Relational aggression among schoolgirls, that is acts intended to hurt others through damaging relationships or threatening one's sense of belonging with others, can include ignoring others, excluding them, sabotaging other relationships that the girl has, or saying she will cut off their relationship if the friend doesn't do what she wants (Centifanti et al., 2015).

Girls also employ indirect aggression, which includes gossiping, spreading rumors, or using others to direct the aggression (Simmons, 2011). Such acts aim to lower a girl's self-esteem, as well as her social status. Given how these alternative aggressions can be practically invisible to the adult eye, they are hard to catch and even harder to prove and punish for (Centifanti et al., 2015). Simmons (2011) believes that one of the most damaging aspects of girls' socialization is that their esteem depends upon relationships and the threat of being isolated or abandoned is paralyzing.

> *Girls enjoy unrestricted access to intimacy. Unlike boys, who are encouraged to separate from their mothers and adopt masculine postures of emotional restraint, girls are urged to identify with the nurturing behavior of their mothers. Girls spend their childhood practicing caretaking and nurturing on each other.* (Simmons, 2011, p. 30)

Female friendships, therefore, can turn into the best weapons of attack, as the girls know each other's intimate secrets and weaknesses. Simmons (2011) believes that because girls are raised to be polite and nice, many have no experience or skill in negotiating conflicts and must resort to destroying relationships in the face of dispute.

Female bullying often is ignored or chalked up to being a phase, rather than being seen for what it is—violence against others. Educators need to keep classroom order and get through a long, daily list of requirements; thus, they triage behaviors and usually mete out punishment for physical, visible acts of aggression (Simmons, 2011). Boys are usually the targets of school discipline as much of girls' bullying is seen less as aggression and more as peer pressure or lack of social skills (Simmons, 2011; Centifanti et al., 2015).

GIRLS' CYBERBULLYING AND CYBERDRAMA

While the virtual world has become the new hangout spot—like the hallway, locker room or cafeteria used to be, "what has changed is the efficiency of aggression: social media is a bathroom wall with a jet engine, giving kids the ability to launch their graffiti into a peer's bedroom or pocket" (Simmon, 2011, p. 104). The internet removes inhibitions; thus, acts of violence that would never take place in face-to-face, public, or even phone exchanges now routinely, openly, and repeatedly occur online.

The online platform offers bullies a stage that is free from perceived morals and often what is said has devastating effects on the recipients (Simmons, 2011). The most recent research shows that females are more likely to be bullied online at 36.6 percent versus 30.5 percent male, while boys are more likely to be the aggressor in virtual bullying at 12.7 percent versus 10.2 percent female (Patchin & Hinduja, 2016).

Simmons (2011) sees girls as particularly unable to handle social media bullying because of their upbringing. Instead of helping them to resolve their problems, social media fans their cruelty; girls are not prepared to address these attacks, given that they are socialized to emotion and caring, rather than conflict resolution through direct means. They are not adept at reading others' exchanges accurately and are more at risk for interpreting them negatively, which deflates their esteem at the same time it may ratchet up hostility and the flow of nasty responses (Simmons, 2011).

There also are interesting personal aspects of both those who are targets and those who are bullies online. Both groups exhibit lower self-esteem than non-bullies. Victims are more prone to anxiety, depression, suicidal ideation, suicide attempts, and school violence (Patchin & Hinduja, 2016). The escalation of emotions that technology now provides is surprising as girls used to be able to stew in their emotions after experiencing a conflict socially, giving them time to process and decide on a reaction, whereas they now move directly into slews of online attacks (Simmons, 2011). Given that transescents and adolescents are in developmental periods in which their brains still have much developing to do, they are poor candidates for gauging the risks they take in launching these cyberattacks (Simmons, 2011).

BULLYING THOSE WITH DISABILITIES

Among ten US studies, there was consistency among the findings that 60 percent of students with disabilities reported being bullied as opposed to 25 percent of their peers (PACER Center, 2016). These same studies show a direct impact upon disabled students' education (PACER Center, 2016; Rose & Gage, 2016). Students with disabilities who are bullied have higher absentee rates, lower grades, more problems with concentration, a loss of interest in their studies, and increased dropout rates (PACER Center, 2016).

Both the Department of Justice and the Office for Civil Rights have written that bullying is also considered harassment, which may involve threats, physical assault, graphic, or written statements, or unwelcome conduct like verbal abuse, name-calling, slurs, or epithets (Gladden et al., 2014). Other conduct that makes a student feel physically threatened or humiliated also may fall into this definition. There are federal laws that protect those with disabilities and all states have addressed bullying in one fashion or another, with some school districts having their own policies (Gladden et al., 2014).

Carter and Spencer (2006) reviewed eleven studies that were conducted from 1989 to 2003; students were categorized by whether their disabilities were visible or not visible to others and determined that both groups of disabled students were more prone to bullying than were their non-disabled counterparts. Dawkins' (1996) study identified four factors predictive of this population being bullied to include being male, having fewer than two good friends, receiving extra school help and being alone at play time. Carter and Spencer (2006) observe that because having a disability made it more likely that students would be in special classes, receive one-to-one help, or be segregated from the mainstream, they were more at risk for being bullied (Carter & Spencer, 2006; Rose & Gage, 2016).

Twyman et al. (2010) reported that children with learning disabilities have a greater risk of becoming victims of bullying but, because of this, they may seek power and status by bullying others. Students who have been identified with other diagnoses that may require educational and/or social interventions are also at greater risk of bullying (Rose & Gage, 2016). Adolescent girls with attention deficit/hyperactivity disorder (ADHD), for example, were hampered more socially than their non-ADHD peers (Sciberras, Ohan, & Anderson, 2011).

In terms of both physical acts and relational interactions, the girls with ADHD suffered from a higher rate of both kinds of incidences, which is illustrative of how schools and communities must address forms of bullying that target students with learning disabilities as well as other special needs that might differentiate them from their peers (Sciberras et al., 2011). This is even more pressing for students who have both disabilities and membership in groups that are marginalized.

The PACER Center (2016) report discovered that adults, including parents, educators, and community members, are the most important advocates for disabled students. While it may be difficult for students with disabilities to talk about bullying and their feelings, adults who adopt a stance of non-judgmental listening, provide emotional safety, and help the students problem solve are in the best position to assist (PACER Center, 2016). Parents should always report incidents of bullying to school staff, and there are letter templates that can be used and tailored to each student's unique situation.

If students with disabilities are bullied, they often feel isolated and alone in their experience. It is essential that students feel surrounded by some individuals that they can immediately turn to—whether they are family, school officials, coaches, mentors, or community members. Disabled students need opportunities to learn how to self-advocate—that is, to speak for themselves, describe their situation, and know their rights. The PACER Center (2016) recommends helping students with action planning and rehearsing ahead of time how they might react to situations. They have materials and resources, as do other organizations that work on behalf of students with disabilities, that can be used to become stronger self-advocates.

Klein (2012) mentions that the cruelty of cyberbullying often extends to those who have the least ability to protect themselves such as students with disabilities. The cyberbullying of those with learning disabilities, speech impediments, or even medical conditions such as multiple sclerosis was visible by teachers, according to Klein (2012). Cyberbullying of those with challenges increases the likelihood of their taking drastic actions, such as staying away from schools, becoming depressed, or even attempting suicide, as children with disabilities often have smaller social networks and fewer personal resources to fight back online.

BULLYING AS A SOCIALLY ACCEPTED NORM IN SCHOOLS

The culture of bullying is seen as perfectly acceptable in many contemporary schools (Bazelon, 2014). According to Bazelon (2014), a popular, female, seventh grade bully, Gianna, felt it a necessary part of the initiation process to bullying new girl, Monique, and measured her as someone who could take it (a perception that would later turn out to be wrong). In bullying Monique, another seventh grader, to the point of her leaving school, Gianna and her friends defend their actions as a mere fact of everyday school life that Monique was not able to understand as "the eighth graders had gunned, flamed, and cracked on them at the beginning of the year, and they'd learned to do it back as a necessity" (Bazelon, 2014, p. 49).

When students do not understand, are not willing, or are not able (perhaps due to cultural barriers or disabilities) to partake in hazing or bullying, they are far more likely to become victims. Bazelon (2014) remarked on how the daily life of the school studied "replicated itself on Facebook . . . the site functioned like a 24/7 parallel combat zone" (p. 50). The biggest page, aptly, was called "Let's Start Drama" and used voting systems around beauty for the girls and fighting for the boys (Bazelon, 2014). After viewing the site Bazelon (2014) understood why girls like Gianna arrived at their perceptions that to survive and to become popular, a level of aggressiveness, not backing away from a fight, either physical or verbal, online or in school, was necessary.

One of the more fascinating distinctions that Gianna and her friends made, though, is that while gunning and cracking were a necessary part of life, one should not crack on those who were weaker or people you did not personally know (Bazelon, 2014). This formed the code by which she and her group functioned, and according to her definition, if you engaged in either of those activities, you were bullying (Bazelon, 2014).

According to the group, they were engaging in drama, which described a broader universe of adolescent behavior as drama withheld judgment about blame and allowed for changes in power dynamics and social status; whereas, the narrower definition of bullying implied an unchanging hierarchy of power (Bazelon, 2014). Seen through this lens, there was much less frequent school bullying than other, adult observers might tally.

Another way in which students differentiate bullying behaviors is illustrated in the case of Phoebe Prince, the South Hadley, Massachusetts student who committed suicide after alleged bullying by classmates. The case received national attention and prompted very different views of what happened, particularly given the reported history of mental health issues and substance use (Bazelon, 2010). The case also highlighted the distinction between what constitutes bullying and dramatic behavior.

The power of verbal abuse can be extremely damaging to a young person's reputation. It is often difficult for adolescents to determine where their behavior is seen as either acceptable or has crossed the line and often they do not figure out that line until they have crossed it and have been called out by others. At that point, whether the behavior being criticized is actual or not, the student's reputation can be irreparably harmed. It is extremely difficult for those being bullied in this fashion to seek adult mediation because of the stigma of sexuality and the fact that adults often feel uncomfortable in intervening in these instances (Bazelon, 2014).

In the case of Jacob, a middle school student in Upstate New York, bullying came as the result of students feeling that he was too "out" in his gay identity (Bazelon, 2014). In a rural setting, discomfort over his open display of his sexual orientation led to verbal and physical abuse that led to serious injury and an eventual lawsuit. But many, including one of his biggest tormentors, felt that the bullying was justified because Jacob was outwardly showing tendencies associated as female instead of keeping his gender preferences to himself (Bazelon, 2014).

Eventually, the principal urged Jacob's family to homeschool him; however, after Jacob received failing grades in three subjects, he reluctantly sought a legal solution to the bullying (Bazelon, 2014). The legal challenges confronting bullied students who take their school systems to court are cumbersome. In the early 1900s principals or schoolmasters were required by law to intervene in bullying of younger pupils by older pupils in instances in which it was likely that physical harm would befall them (Bazelon, 2014).

They also were tasked with vigilant supervision so that misconduct could be anticipated.

Courts, however, were lax in enforcing the duty of anticipating danger, leaving the decision making to school administrators and de facto preventing many bullied students from legal recourse (Bazelon, 2014; Cornell & Limber, 2016). At this point in history, a bullied student must be able to prove that he or she has suffered discrimination—that the bullying has deprived him or her of equal rights (the Fourteenth Amendment). It was not until 1993 that the first gay student used this route (Bazelon, 2014; Cornell & Limber, 2016).

Jamie Nabozny, a gay Wisconsin seventeen-year-old, had been verbally and physically attacked to the point that he attempted suicide four times during middle and high school (Terry, 1996). Attacks included a mock rape in front of an entire science class, as well as kickings and beatings that caused the need for abdominal surgery (Terry, 1996).

When his parents confronted the school teacher, she told them, "I can't make the entire school different for your son. He has to expect trouble if he behaves this way" (Bazelon, 2014, p. 147). Later, in court, it was confirmed that she had told him that he shouldn't go around expressing his sexual preference, leading to the court's decision to award damages. The school district settled for damages and medical expenses before this phase of the trial could be reached (Associated Press, 1996). Jacob's case was concluded in his favor, but in most cases, school districts, perpetrators, and their families remained relatively impenitent about the way they had treated the plaintiffs, claiming often that this was because the Bible taught that homosexuality was a sin (Bazelon, 2014).

In one of the most heinous cases of school hazing, a student was stripped, taped to a bench, beaten until bleeding, and sexually assaulted; this took place in the football locker room while more than a dozen coaches were present or in the vicinity (Ward, 2004). When the family pressed charges, the school community turned on them. "After the incident, we were considered dirt, we were spit at," the mother recounts; "People told her, 'Why don't you just let it go?'" (Klein, 2012, p. 140).

ADULTS AS BULLIES

Sadly, children and adolescents are not the only bullies in the school community. Klein (2012) noted that teachers, school personnel, and parents also can bully children and each other. The memoir of Brooks Brown, who was friends with Columbine shooter Dylan Klebold, shows that, at times, teachers were no better than their pupils when it came to ridicule and mocking young people:

> *The mean-spirited hierarchy, writes Brooks, was replayed in one way or another by those who had the most power in school—teachers, coaches and principals, as well as those referred to as jocks. They often seemed to take it for granted that the less popular students would be treated badly.* (Klein, 2012, p. 128)

School Staff

There are many forms of adult bullying that take place in schools; some are passive—such as ignoring, condoning, or dismissing youth bullying against certain populations (Klein, 2012). Others blame this stance on the need for kids to "toughen up" in order to prepare to enter the adult world. Some adults are more active bullies, targeting students and humiliating them or boxing them into narrow gender roles or stereotypes (Klein, 2012). They often model these same behaviors in the treatment of peers at school, openly or subtly making comments or acting in ways that clearly demonstrate gender, racial, religious, ethnic, or sexual orientation biases. Parents often suffer the same fate and

> *are so used to bullying behavior that they simply don't see it—and when they do, many think that it is normal. A parent will call another mother and say, "Little Joey is picking on my son on the bus. He's calling my son nasty names and my son is very upset." And it is not unusual to hear from that parent: Oh, well, that's just kids, what's the big deal, its just boys being boys.* (Klein, 2012, p. 129)

Adult staff in the schools often simply believe that those who are the targets of bullies are children who don't know how to handle others. In the face of such adult attitudes, bullied students may simply give up, assuming that there is no recourse. There also are disparate perceptions of adult intervention; for example, Klein (2012) cited an ABC news special in which researchers discovered an act of bullying every eight minutes on the playground. While teachers told the researchers that they intervened "all the time," the researchers' observations documented that they acted in fewer than 5 percent of the incidents of bullying (Klein, 2012). Low-level harassment that does not involve more violent actions often flies under the radar and children and adolescents often are ashamed or humiliated to report that they have been bullied, for fear of being singled out as a tattletale or making the bullying worse.

Coaches, Parents, and Sporting Events

In other venues, such as sports, adults may willingly or inadvertently, promote hypermasculine or even violent behaviors. While school administrators are likely to see "outsider" students, such as "Goths," as more likely candidates for bullying others, high-status students such as the "jocks" actually commit more daily abuse (Klein, 2012).

Athletic cultures allow coaches an extraordinary amount of power to display hypermasculine behaviors in the service of building character, team cohesiveness, and the toughness necessary to compete; this often spills over into girls' sports, as well, since athletic coaches still tend to be male, and most female coaches were coached by males themselves (Gibson & O'Gorman, 2017). Despite some recent, high-profile national cases, a good deal of hazing still attends initiation into sports teams at the middle and high school levels. Allan and Madden (2008) found that 25 percent of students who were involved in hazing said their coaches were aware of the activity and 22 percent took part in it personally. Designed to build camaraderie and toughness, these actions serve to normalize bullying behavior instead (Gibson & O'Gorman, 2017).

In the case of the Columbine shootings, members of various boys' athletic teams openly explained to the press why they taunted the shooters and others they considered to act outside of the mainstream of the school's values and behaviors.

Most members of the 'in group' considered taunting the 'outsiders' a reasonable thing to do. Aronson quotes one member of the Columbine football team, who said, 'Columbine is a good, clean place except for those rejects. Most kids didn't want them there. Sure we teased them. But what do you expect with kids who come to school with weird hairdos and horns on their hats? It's not just the jocks; the whole school's disgusted with them...If you want to get rid of someone, usually you tease 'em. So the whole school would call them homos. (Klein, 2012, p. 15)

There is huge pressure on school sports teams to win because so many parents and students believe that youth sports are their ticket to college recruitment and scholarships (Gibson & O'Gorman, 2017). This makes it more likely to ignore bullying behaviors. Coaches may use bullying to create a hierarchy on the team, with designated student-athletes tasked to serve as surrogates in reinforcing desired behaviors (Gibson & O'Gorman, 2017). Parents frequently act in bullying ways at school sporting events, yelling at or demeaning those who do not succeed and acting aggressively toward both their own children and others.

Parents

Cohn and Canter (2003) report on the myriad ways in which adults directly or indirectly influence bullying behaviors. These include acting overtly as bullies themselves, mandating no consequences at home when children are bullied, and failing to intervene when they are bystanders. Parents also may use corporal punishment or verbal threats or humiliation to discipline their own children; deprived of feelings of esteem and respect at home the children find power and status by bullying others at school (Klein, 2012).

Parents may also become the bully believing that it can be condoned, in part, because they are subjected to these behaviors at work or in their own lives (Evans & Thompson, 2016). One mother related the importance of money and sports as status symbols in her community saying, "parents push their children really hard, but they also bully other parents to make sure their children get to play" (Klein, 2012, p. 130). Aggressive behavior can be seen as the norm and parents who perceive they have power and status in the community wield it, frequently in ways that parallel those of young bullies (Evans & Thompson, 2016). It is not surprising then, that bullying behavior most often begins at home.

According to Evans and Thompson (2016), there are three kinds of parent-bullies that can initiate problems with school administration and teachers to include the following:

- Righteous Crusader: Attacks the school or teacher for a perceived moral injustice that often does not exist.
- Vicious Gossip: Exaggerates issues and finds continual fault with school or teachers and shares with anyone who will listen to the point of destruction.
- Entitled Intimidator: Demands special treatment for child including waiving rules and policies, as well as making exceptions when needed (n.p.).

At some events, parents have even acted violently against other parents at the same school; in the famous case in Massachusetts, one father beat another to death at a hockey game while their sons were witnesses (Gubar, 2015). In Philadelphia, a father pulled a gun on his son's football coach because he felt that he wasn't giving him enough playing time (Gubar, 2015).

Students

Adults who are consciously or unconsciously a part of a bullying culture are both perpetrators and often victims of the same cruel behavior to which students are subjected.

Klein (2012) also notes that teachers may be bullied by their students such as an Asian American middle school teacher being treated in a derogatory fashion by her class, particularly because she spoke with an accent and pronounced some words differently. The classroom bullying led to her resignation early into her first year of teaching (Klein, 2012). In another case, a female teacher who taught in an all-male prep school recalled being bullied by the boys, who shouted her down in class, acted out with physical violence, and repeatedly doodled penises on their homework assignments (Klein, 2012).

BULLYING THE LGBTQ+ COMMUNITY IN SCHOOLS

As long as there have been formal schools, social pressure has been part of the experience of many students, regardless of their sexual orientation or gender identity. Yet, LGBTQ+ students often struggle to piece together their identities and may face backlash or misunderstanding from family and friends. They encounter hostile messages about LGBTQ+ people at school, church, and in their community, and social pressures may be well beyond what most others feel (Kosciw et al., 2016). The 2013 National School Climate Survey (Kosciw et al., 2016) found that over half of all LGBTQ+ students reported feeling unsafe at their schools and the epidemic of aggression against school-aged students in the LGBTQ+ community is at a record high (Lang, 2018).

In most school communities, LGBTQ+ students are more likely than heterosexual peers to suffer abuse (Thoreson, 2016). One transgender student in Utah stated that school administrators dismissed his complaints of verbal and physical abuse, blaming him for being "so open about it" (Thoreson, 2016, n.p.). In some cases, it was the teachers themselves who bullied the LGBTQ+ youth or joined the bullying as in the case of a young girl with a gay father in South Dakota, whose mother recounted how when her daughter was eight, "she ran home because they were teasing her. . . . She saw a teacher laughing and that traumatized her even worse" (Thoreson, 2016, n.p.).

Discrimination against transgender students comes in many forms, including restricting bathroom and locker room use, limiting participation in extracurricular activities, and other forms of expression—for example, dressing for the school day or special events like homecoming. "They didn't let me in and I didn't get my money back," said one transgender girl who attempted to wear a dress to her homecoming (Thoreson, 2016, n.p.).

LGBTQ+ students described persistent patterns of isolation, exclusion, and marginalization that made them feel unsafe or unwelcome at school. The use of slurs, lacking resources relevant to their experience, being discouraged from having same-sex relationships, and being regularly misgendered made the school a hostile environment, which in turn may impact student health and well-being (Thoreson, 2016).

Thoreson's (2016) research, conducted over a year in five diverse states, utilized semi-structured, qualitative interviews to capture the daily school experiences of the LGBTQ+ population. At the time of the study, only twenty states had anti-bullying laws on their books that prohibited the bullying of students on the bases of sexual orientation and gender identity and eight states actually had laws restricting teachers and school personnel from discussing LGBTQ+ issues in school (Thoreson, 2016). The CDC 2016 Youth at Risk Behavior Survey found that 42.8 percent of LGBTQ+ youth had seriously considered suicide in the previous year and almost 30 percent had attempted it, compared with 14.8 and 6.4 percent of heterosexual students.

The 2013 study found that of LGBTQ+ students, 74 percent were verbally bullied and 36 percent were physically bullied for their sexual orientation, while 55 percent were verbally bullied and 23 percent were physically bullied for their gender expression. For all LGBTQ+ students, 49 percent had experienced cyberbullying (Kosciw, Greytak, Palmer, & Boesen, 2013). More than one-third of LGBTQ+ students surveyed felt unsafe at school due to their gender expression, while more than one half felt the same way due to their sexual orientation (Kosciw et al., 2013).

Gay bashing is most likely to be ignored (or in some cases, even condoned) because of the high degree of homophobia among adults and adults often blamed the victim, saying that LGBTQ+ students who were open about their orientation were "flaunting" and should expect that others might react against them (Klein, 2012). A double standard existed, however, in that these same adults rarely stepped in if boys were bragging openly about their sexual exploits with girls (Klein, 2012).

Gay bashing obviously includes bullying of people who openly identify as part of the LGBTQ+ community, yet it seeps over into attacks on boys who are perceived to lack hypermasculine qualities or girls who appear to have them (Kimmel, 2014). Klein (2012) reports that more than 75 percent of students who were surveyed heard homophobic slurs "frequently" or "often" while at school. Additional statistics show that 44 percent had heard them from "most of their peers" and 19 percent had heard them from staff or teachers (Klein, 2012, p. 83). The average high school student hears 25 anti-gay slurs per day (Klein, 2012). Even generalized slurs contribute to a sense of hostility and danger in a school culture (Thoreson, 2016). The fact that such bullying targets both gay-identified and heterosexual youth reveals the extent of the problem.

Cyberbullying of the LGBTQ+ community can cross multiple boundaries in its cruelty and one student recalled the torment of being assigned to use the eighth grade boys' locker room for gym, having to strip down into her female underwear in front of the boys, and told that she could not use the girls' locker room to change; eventually, she was assaulted by a group of football players while in the locker room (Klein, 2012).

Bullying also takes a toll on lesbian and bisexual girl students, who were frequently targeted by boys who asked them to have a threesome or perform sex with their girlfriends while the boys watched (Thoreson, 2016). While gay and bisexual boys were not generally treated as sex objects, the same could not be said for the girls in these populations, and they often were propositioned for sex by straight male peers.

A gender-fluid student talked about how "people would just grab my butt or my boobs or my crotch" to see if they were "real" (Klein, 2012, p. 33). When such students went to their teachers the most common response was that of a brush-off; however, teachers did intervene, according to the interviewees, if they saw same-sex couples openly displaying affection (Klein, 2012). While teachers ignored such displays in heterosexual couples, the same teachers intervened and disciplined when the couples were homosexual, often telling them that it was a "sin" and outing them to their parents (Klein, 2012).

BULLYING OF TEACHERS

The hierarchical bullying that occurs against students also occurs among school faculty (Klein, 2012). There are many levels of power within a school and adults can act in bullying manners against those who have less status; for example, new teachers are at the low end of the chain of command; when they rise in power, they may treat novices in the ways that they were treated.

Administrators have more power than teachers, and in locales where sports reign supreme, coaches may have almost more power than anyone. Conditions of hazing, bullying, and "pulling rank" may drive promising new educators out of the profession as the most fragile, least-experienced teachers usually are given the most difficult posts (Klein, 2012). Reflecting on her own twelve years in a large, public, New York City secondary school, Klein (2012) wrote that when teachers were treated poorly by their supervisors, they tended to inflict the same hostility on their students and lower-level peers.

Bullied adults are similar to bullied students; those who have been bullied are more apt to become bullies themselves, feeling that they have no other recourse to claiming some modicum of respect and power (Finley, 2013). As it does with students, adult school bullying maintains a pecking order with the abuse moving down the chain of command (Finley, 2013).

In some cases, the image of toughness that adults try to portray to their students is intimidating to other adults in the building. This may include verbally abusive behavior, demeaning others in public, or symbols that are displayed. The experiences that adults in schools underwent help to perpetuate the bully culture; the harsh lessons that they were subjected to in school may still apply (Finley, 2013). If they bullied to rise to the top, or if they were bullied and were at the bottom of the heap—these experiences shape their adult psychology (Finley, 2013).

The cycle of bullying from teachers to students, and from students to teachers, is integrally linked to a larger bully culture in which aggressive actions are seen as the means for getting ahead in life (Klein, 2012). The private Horace Mann School in New York City became the subject of an internal and external debate about cyberbullying when a teacher at the school stumbled across troubling Facebook groups; one was a Men's Issues Group dedicated to sexually derogatory behavior against women and another was devoted to denigrating a female teacher at the school (Winig, 2015). While the use of cyber sites to vent against faculty was not uncommon,

> *These Facebook pages, however, were something different. Kids have always ragged on an unpopular teacher or ridiculed an unfortunate classmate. But sites like Facebook and RateMyTeachers.com are changing the power dynamics of the community in an unpredictable way. It is as if students were standing outside the classroom window, taunting the teacher to her face.* (Sherman, 2008, p. 1)

The incidents at Horace Mann School, a school attended by children of the rich and famous, are seen by some as a clash of high-status families and the lower social-status teachers (Sherman, 2008). As Klein (2012) remarks, "The wealthier children bully their less wealthy teachers in a disturbing class war that is also replayed among the students over more minor class differences" (p. 145). This behavior seemed to be woven into the very fabric of the school, but whether this constituted actual bullying or not was disputed by those in authority. The exchange below, between the teacher who was targeted, and a Trustee, attempting to excuse the students' behavior, illustrates just how fraught the definition and issue of cyberbullying is:

> *"Students are just blowing off steam," the trustee said. "They're very stressed; it's not unusual for them to say racist and sexist things ... The site is private."*
>
> *"No," McGuire insisted, "it's got 9 million users."*
>
> *"What you did was like breaking into my daughter's room and reading her diary. . ."*
>
> *"No," McGuire said, the emotion rising in her voice, "what your daughter did was the equivalent of posting something in Times Square." (Sherman, 2008, p. 4)*

FINAL THOUGHTS

Schools, which should be safe havens for both students and adults alike, often are plagued by bully cultures in which individuals attempt to gain power and status through the use of physical, verbal, and electronic bullying. The forms of bullying run the gamut from teasing and name calling to threatening, taunting, or using physical force or acts of violence against the target. With increasingly sophisticated means of electronic harassment and bullying, the scope and timing of these acts is limitless. Students who are bullied can literally be under siege all of the time. The stress of being bullied intensifies and in some cases leads to depression or suicidal thoughts or actions, while in others, it can ratchet up into additional violent actions.

Certain students and groups appear to be more likely targets of bullying in American schools. These include groups that are considered to be on the margins of mainstream school culture. The most vulnerable are those with any kind of disabilities, physical appearance, economic status, religion, race, ethnicity, or sexual orientation that are deemed "atypical" by the majority school culture. Those wishing to attain higher status and power target those they perceive to be less powerful to be their victims. In many cases, bullies actually are bullied themselves. There tends to be a social and family influence on the creation and perpetuation of bullies and bully culture, where acting out with verbal or physical aggression against others is normalized.

Adults frequently model bullying behavior in their homes, but it is even more upsetting to recognize that teachers, staff, and administrators may bully certain types of students in school. This may be expressed in active terms or by refusing to intervene when bullying occurs. It also can take the form of implying to victims that they somehow deserve the bullying because of their lifestyle "choices" or that they simply need to "toughen up" and the bullying will stop.

Adults within school buildings may bully each other, and parents or community members may turn on teachers or coaches if they feel that their children have been wronged. This bullying behavior can be the result of grades, playing time, or perceived injustices and can be expressed in verbal, physical, or electronic harassment.

Until schools become places in which all constituents can feel safe, accepted, and valued, the bully culture will continue. Fortunately, there are promising practices that can be instituted to promote more inclusive, respectful learning communities.

POINTS TO REMEMBER

- *Bullying can be defined as repeatedly exposing the victim to a variety of physical or relational acts of aggression. It can be conducted face-to-face or in cyberspace and ranges from teasing and name calling to threatening, taunting, or acting against the victim with physical violence.*
- *Bullying takes different shapes depending on one's gender: boys tend to use more physical, aggressive means, whereas girls use more subtle, relational forms, such as social isolation, gossiping and rumor mongering, and exclusion from groups or events.*
- *Certain groups of students are more likely to be the targets of bullying, including those with disabilities, members of the LGBTQ+ community, and other marginalized groups.*
- *Ongoing bullying of an individual can lead to anxiety, depression, missed days of school, poor grades, social isolation, and physical and mental health issues, as well as pent-up anger and rage.*

Chapter 4

What We See Is What We Get

The Role of Society and the Media in School Violence

Research shows that school violence stems from a layering of causes and risk factors that include access to weapons, media violence, cyber abuse, the impact of school, community, and family environments, and personal alienation (Constitutional Rights Foundation, 2018). While overall crime rates in the United States have fallen, school violence and violent behaviors have increased (Constitutional Rights Foundation, 2018). In the first half of academic year 2014–2015, Trump (2014) reviewed 812 school threats across the country and determined that school-based threats of violence increased by 158 percent from the prior year.

School and public safety officials must treat these threats seriously and have established protocols in place for the assessment and management of threats to school safety. It is critical that school officials follow emergency guidelines as they assist school administrators in making cognitive decisions based on the facts of the actual threat (Trump, 2014). It is important that schools have previously developed crisis communication plans for distributing accurate information in a timely manner to parents, the media, and the wider community when rumors and threats occur, effectively eliminating incorrect reporting that causes undue stress (Trump, 2018).

It is essential that school leaders establish a threat assessment protocol to ensure consistency and thoroughness when evaluating and responding to threats against a school. Threat assessment procedures should involve analyzing the behavior process of the person making the threat instead of using a profile based on a set of specific characteristics as criteria (Trump, 2018).

During the threat assessment process, schools should ask a common set of questions for each threat received. Schools should inquire about the motivation of the individual making the threat, the credibility of the threat, whether the individual has the information and tools to carry out the threat, and whether the person has the capability of actually carrying it out (Trump, 2018). When assessing the credibility of a threat, crisis teams should focus on the behavioral actions toward planning and carrying out the threat, not just the details and specificity of the threat (Trump, 2018). The more details and specifics contained in the threat, particularly the evidence of planning and action steps to carry out the threat, the more credible the threat (Trump, 2014).

THREAT ESCALATION

Threats of school violence are often made with the intent of disrupting education and the number of threats generally increases in the spring due to media-fed awareness of high-profile tragedies and the resultant frustration and anger in the spring of those students that have been bullied throughout an unsuccessful school year (Trump, 2014).

Advances in modern communication also escalate the number of threats that occur, particularly after a school shooting is carried out (Harding, 2018). Research shows that four to six weeks after an initial incident, there is an increase in school threats due to students' use of poor judgment and/or because they feel they can identify with the perpetrator's anger or sense of isolation (Harding, 2018).

The use of social media also has the potential to trigger crisis, increase the perception of threats and fear, or create a contagion effect where learning about one crisis leads to another (National Association of School Psychologists [NASP], 2016a). According to a recent study, more than one-third of violent threats to schools were delivered by social media, email, and text messaging (Trump, 2014). Research has found that text messages and cell phones create more anxiety among students than any actual threats or incidents that may have triggered the rumors (Trump, 2014).

THREAT MANAGEMENT

The widespread availability of social media allows rumors to be spread like wildfire and school officials must have a solid crisis communications plan to manage rapidly escalating rumors around school safety issues (Trump, 2014). To counteract rumors and school violence threats in a timely manner, school officials must release accurate information as soon as possible as well provide periodic updates as necessary and appropriate (Trump, 2014). It is imperative that school officials also publicize the same information on parent alert systems, social media, text messaging, school website, letters sent home, and mass media (Trump, 2014). Any messages sent by the school must also be in line and consistent with those sent by public safety officials (Trump, 2014).

To manage threats, text messages, and rumors of school violence and the rapid spread of fear, Trump (2014) recommends that schools anticipate that an issue will arise that will rapidly spread at some point in their school and identify the strategies beforehand that will be used to counter it. Administrators and crisis teams should discuss potential scenarios to evaluate at what point a situation might rise to the level of being disruptive or distracting that it warrants schools to forge ahead full speed with communication efforts (Miller, 2014). Communication consultants and district communication personnel can help develop communication plans and train school staff on effective methods of communication with the media and students' parents (Miller, 2014).

Solid legal and administrative provisions for discipline should be included in school board policies and student policies and handbooks that address students who make threats or send text messages that are disruptive to the educational process (Trump, 2014). It is also important to educate students on behavioral expectations related to preventing and reporting rumors and threats of violence during a crisis situation (Miller, 2014). Students should be made aware that responsible behavior is expected and that there are consequences for inappropriate behavior that could potentially compromise school safety, such as starting, spreading, and fueling rumors (Trump, 2014). Teachers should have procedures in place for notifying administrators and security personnel regarding students' misuse of cell phones and texting in the classroom and common areas (Trump, 2014).

SOCIAL MEDIA AND THE PREVENTION
OF SCHOOL VIOLENCE

Research indicates that as many as 90 percent of 13–17-year-olds use some form of social media, which allows school administrators, teachers, parents, and law enforcement officials widely available insight into the thought process of a perpetrator and his or her plans to commit an act of violence in the form of leakage, or hints, and potentially help violent incidents from occurring (Agrawal, 2017; NASP, 2016a). These messages and threats are signals for help and should always be taken seriously (Agrawal, 2017). During times of crisis, students can use various forms of social media to provide live updates, particularly to let friends and family know they are safe (Agrawal, 2017). After violent incidents occur, social media can be, and often is, used as a space for venting and expression of frustration (Agrawal, 2017).

Social Media Risks

Social media has many associated risks and can contribute to the psychological trauma of students who experience bullying or violent acts. Through cyberbullying, students can experience widespread and direct public ridicule, and schools with their own social media sites may find users who adopt false profiles and/or post negative comments (NASP, 2016b). While schools that use social media on a consistent basis can benefit by becoming aware of online conflicts, and traumatic, embarrassing, or inappropriate information, administrators and crisis response teams can grapple with determining who is responsible for monitoring the posts and the issues they present (NASP, 2016b).

Social media allows for the quick and widespread dissemination of information. While this can be a benefit in certain situations, it can also perpetuate the spreading of crisis-related rumors or other false information as well as embarrassing or inappropriate information (O'Keefe & Clarke-Pearson, 2011). More importantly, the overuse of social media and its role as a consistent substitute for face-to-face socializing may put students at risk for sharing too much information, leaving themselves vulnerable to perpetrators, privacy issues, and social media depression (NASP, 2016b).

With social media platforms and applications evolving at a lightning fast pace, it is difficult and time-consuming for educators and parents to stay informed on what virtual applications students are using, much less learning the social media platform and monitoring student use (O'Keefe & Clarke-Pearson, 2011). Avoiding social media altogether will not eliminate the risks of its use and may actually lead to the perception that the school is failing to communicate (NASP, 2016).

Social Media Benefits

Crisis Prevention

The use of social media can encourage positive behavior, responsibility, and healthy relationships in schools, homes, and in the community (NASP, 2016b). By posting positive messages or achievements on social media, students can create an extended sense of community or culture and open a place for diverse audiences to connect (O'Keefe & Clarke-Pearson, 2011). Online surveillance and monitoring for crisis warning signs or threats, can also be conducted through social media sites such as Facebook, who has partnered with the National Suicide Prevention Lifeline to create a suicide reporting mechanism (NASP, 2016b).

Crisis Intervention

Social media has the capability of quickly communicating accurate information following a crisis, rapidly dispelling any rumors or false information associated with the event and coordinating crisis response efforts in a timely manner (Trump, 2018). Students who may be affected by a crisis situation can be evaluated or triaged quickly for any warning signs and crisis prevention resources can be disseminated immediately, such as how students can access mental health services (NASP, 2016a).

SCHOOL SAFETY AND CRISIS RESPONSE PLANNING

With the increased number of social media users spanning across all age groups, schools would benefit from creating and implementing policies and plans around social media use. Social media is easy to use and can provide an alternative or supplemental way for schools to disseminate crisis-related information quickly and in real time (Asher, 2015). Benefits of using social media for crisis response work include the ability for school administrators to remotely post updates, facilitate discussions, provide support and resource options, and increase community perceptions of the school's caring and helpful culture (Trump, 2018).

Prior to Using Social Media

According to the US Department of Education's Office of Safe and Healthy Students, schools should set social media goals and objectives, develop policies, and plan ahead before implementing any form of social media (NASP, 2016a). In setting social media goals and objectives, school administrators and crisis response team members must determine who is the intended audience, how the use of social media will complement any existing communication strategies, and what types of information will be conveyed and received on social media sites (NASP, 2016a).

When developing policies related to social media, schools must determine who will be responsible for communicating crisis-related information via social media (i.e., a social media manager) (Asher, 2015). This designated official can then collaborate with school administrators and public information officers to ensure the release of valid and factual information and monitor social media during and after any incidents (NASP, 2016b). It is critical that schools also create and prominently display a social media comment policy for community users that makes them aware that all comments will be deleted that contain profanity, hate speech, defamation, and so on (Thompson et al., 2016).

During the planning stage, discussions should include collaboration between school administrators, the school's public information officer, and any other partnering agencies, such as the local fire, police, and/or health departments (NASP, 2016b; Trump, 2014). It is recommended that schools choose not only a primary social media platform that will reach the majority of users in the target audience, but a secondary platform that may capture the remaining users (Thompson et al., 2016).

To build a sustainable, comprehensive, and consistent following on social media sites, schools should integrate crisis information with general, engaging school content, such as video and discussion options (NASP, 2016b). Without a sizeable number of users and consistent and effective use, social media communications may be unnoticed, overlooked, or even disregarded, leading to a loss of user confidence and interest (NASP, 2016b).

Without prior planning for the monitoring of social media comments and addressing feedback, users may become dissatisfied or disconnected. Having outdated, unappealing, or irrelevant information posted on a school's social media site may lead to negative perceptions of the school and can lead users to block, unfollow, or simply ignore the site (NASP, 2016). Schools must also recognize and plan for language, socioeconomic, and other barriers that may prevent parents and other individuals from accessing the school's social media (Thompson et al., 2016).

SOCIAL MEDIA PRACTICES

When planning high-quality school emergency operations, the US Department of Education recommends specific areas that can be integrated with social media to create more effective school crisis safety and intervention efforts (NASP, 2016b).

Prevention

It is essential that schools post notices to parents and other community members with instructions on how to get important information from the school's social media sites (NASP, 2016b). Information on crises prevention, safety planning efforts, family reunification plan, and procedures in the event of an early release and/or a crisis situation should all be readily available and easily accessible. Schools should predetermine who will be responsible for reviewing and updating any social media, including the school's policy and procedure guidelines on social media usage (Thompson et al., 2016).

Social media is an excellent way for schools to send positive messages that reinforce a safe and caring school climate and should consider speaking with students for cultural insight on how social media is being, and should be, used within the school culture (Thompson, 2016).

Protection

Schools should continuously monitor their social media sites to determine if any unknown problems exist and identify potentially valuable information missing from the social media platform (NASP, 2016b). Media sites should also be constantly monitored for dangerous information, inappropriate comments, and/or particular key words that suggest a violent situation may be impending (NASP, 2016b). Schools may consider using specific web-based applications to notify administrators and officials when inappropriate information is posted online as well as creating an anonymous reporting system for students (Thompson et al., 2016).

Mitigation

Through the use of social media, schools can reframe any challenging situations or negative comments that were posted and reach out to individuals, if known, to suggest further conversations, if needed (NASP, 2016b). Accurate and appropriate information regarding a crisis situation can be distributed as quickly as possible while simultaneously respecting student/family privacy (Thompson et al., 2016).

Response

Hashtags can be used to help track crisis event information quickly, monitor comments related to an event, or evaluate individual student needs. Links to helpful, factual information, guidelines, school safety policies, and crisis procedures can also be retweeted (Thompson et al., 2016).

Recovery

After an incident occurs, times, dates, and locations of in-person community informational gatherings, memorials, and other outreach efforts can be posted as well as any available updates, such as school reopening procedures, and celebrations of positive recovery steps, such as volunteer thank-you's and photos (NASP, 2016b; Thompson et al., 2016).

ROLE OF SOCIETY IN SCHOOL VIOLENCE

In today's society, students are more likely to grow up with parents who abuse drugs, get arrested, go to prison, disappear, fail to maintain stable families, and live in poverty (Constitutional Rights Foundation, 2018). Research shows that students who are exposed to these and other risk factors are more likely to act out with violent behavior (Constitutional Rights Foundation, 2018; Simckes, 2017; Enyinnaya, 2018).

Access to Weapons

Students' access to guns, either in their own home, friends' homes, or school, can increase their risk of becoming a victim, for committing a violent crime, including suicide and homicide, and for experiencing an unintentional injury or death (Simckes, 2017). Research shows that approximately 35 percent of US homes with children under age 18 have at least one firearm which translates into 11 million children living in homes with firearms (Constitutional Rights Foundation, 2108). This increased access to guns along with other factors such as gang presence in schools, unsecured guns in the home, and prior victimization, may leave students at a remarkably high risk of self-inflicted injury and perpetration of interpersonal violence (Simckes, 2017).

Of the 10,704 students between the ages of 12 and 18 that responded to the school crime supplement of the National Crime Victimization Survey in 2011 and 2013, 4 percent of the students said they could get access to a loaded gun without adult permission (Simckes, 2017). A more recent health study conducted by the National Institute of Health interviewed 1,219 students in seventh and tenth grades in Boston, MA, and Milwaukee, WI, and found that 42 percent of students could readily obtain a gun if they wanted, 28 percent had handled a gun without adult knowledge or supervision, and 17 percent had carried a concealed gun (Constitutional Rights Foundation, 2018).

Current evidence suggests that students who have been the victims of bullying and cyberbullying by their peers are particularly vulnerable to gun violence and are more likely to carry guns more often than non-bullied students (Simckes, 2017; Lurie, 2014). Overall, students that have been bullied are three times more likely to report that they could get access to a loaded gun compared to their non-bullied peers (Simckes, 2017). More specifically, those students who experienced only traditional bullying were two times more likely and students reporting only cyberbullying were three times more likely, and students who experienced both types of bullying were six times more likely to have access to a loaded gun (Simckes, 2017; Lurie, 2014).

Another study revealed that 20 percent of the respondents admitted to being victims of bullying and those students were substantially more likely to carry weapons if they had experienced one or more risk factors, such as feeling unsafe at school, having property stolen/damaged, participating in a fight within the last year, and/or having been threatened or injured by a weapon (Lurie, 2014). Among the respondents that had experienced all of these risk factors, 72 percent had personally brought a weapon to school and 63 percent had carried a gun, making them 50 times more likely to bring a weapon to school than those students who were not victims of bullying (Lurie, 2014).

Substance Abuse

Although there is limited research on the connection between substance abuse and school violence, the research that has been done indicates there is a strong relationship between school violence and drug use in young adults (Ramorola & Joyce, 2014). One study, for example, found that more than 200,000 teenagers between the ages of 12 and 17 used drugs; as a result, these students also took more risks, were more likely to carry weapons, engaged in more fights, and were more likely to become victims of violence (Ramorola & Joyce, 2014). Being under the influence of substance and alcohol abuse also caused students to lose control of their inhibitions and act in an irrational manner, serving as a catalyst for school violence (Enyinnaya, 2018).

Violence in the Media and Cyber Abuse

Evidence shows that by the time the average American student reaches the seventh grade, they will have witnessed 8,000 murders and 100,000 acts of violence just on television alone (Constitutional Rights Foundation, 2018). There has been a continual debate among society whether watching violence on television actually causes students to become more violent (Enyinnaya, 2018). Research is increasingly supporting the idea that exposure to violence in the media increases the likelihood of physically and verbally abusive behavior as students will often emulate their favorite television or video game character (Constitutional Rights Foundation, 2018; Enyinnaya, 2018).

Today's video games feature high levels of realistic violence and research on the effects of exposure show that students who have more exposure to violent video games hold more pro-violent attitudes, more hostile personalities, are less forgiving, believe violence is normal, and behave more aggressively (Constitutional Rights Foundation, 2018).

Environment

Race and ethnicity, income levels, substance abuse, and other measurable variables only partially explain adolescent health risk behaviors such as bullying and violence. Research has discovered that students' immediate environments, including their school, community, peer group, and family can exert a powerful influence on attitudes and behaviors (Bowes, Arsenault, Maughan, Taylor, Caspi, & Moffitt, 2009).

One recent survey found that almost 50 percent of all teenagers, regardless of their settings believe their schools are becoming more violent (Constitutional Rights Foundation, 2018). School enrollment size has been found to be directly correlated with discipline problems with large schools yielding more discipline problems than small schools (Constitutional Rights Foundation, 2018). In a recent survey, 34 percent of schools with 1,000 or more students reported student assaults on teachers at least once per week, compared with 21 percent of those at schools with 500–999 students, 17 percent of those at schools with 300–499 students, and 14 percent of those at schools with less than 300 students (Constitutional Rights Foundation, 2018).

Adolescence is a transition phase between childhood and adulthood that is characterized by physical, psychological, and emotional and social changes and can result in experimentation in activities such as smoking and alcohol and drug use (Ramorola & Joyce, 2014). During adolescence, students are also faced with personal vulnerability in that they face changes within themselves, their family dynamics, and in their social interactions with others (Ramorola & Joyce, 2014).

Collectively, these experiences during adolescence are a contributing factor in middle school students being more than twice as likely as high school students to be affected by school violence (Constitutional Rights Foundation, 2018). Early adolescence, hyperactivity, the lack of knowledge regarding acceptable social behavior and, for some, the first contact with students from different backgrounds all contribute to the increased rate of middle school violence (Constitutional Rights Foundation, 2018; Bowles et al., 2009).

Although there are certain risk factors that can make some students more vulnerable to victimization and perpetration and contribute to the likelihood of student violence occurring, they are not the direct cause of violence (Bowles et al., 2009; Centers for Disease Control and Preventions, 2018). Some students that become violent are following behavior they have observed at home, in their neighborhoods, or in video games, movies, or television while other students are victims of bullying that have reached their limit and feel violence is their only way to make the victimization stop (Bowles et al., 2009).

Social and peer risk factors can include involvement in gangs, social rejection by peers, poor academic performance, and low commitment to school and school failure (Centers for Disease Control and Prevention,

2018). The community a student lives within also has its own set of risk factors as high concentrations of poor residents, low levels of community participation, and socially disorganized neighborhoods can all contribute to a student's propensity for violence (Centers for Disease Control and Prevention, 2018).

School violence can also be the result of psychological deficiencies created by dysfunctional homes (Enyinnaya, 2018). Students can develop worry, hatred, an inferiority complex, anger and other negative emotions that fuel violent behavior as a result of exposure to poor parenting or disagreement among family members. In homes where parents display violent behavior, children typically adopt violence as their way of asserting authority (Enyinnaya, 2018). Other family risk factor that contribute to student violence include harsh, lax or inconsistent disciplinary practices, low parental involvement, low emotional attachment to parents, and poor monitoring and supervision of children (Centers for Disease Control and Prevention, 2018).

FINAL THOUGHTS

School violence is a result of many underlying causes and risk factors that span from the students' school environment and experiences to their home life and exposure to negative behaviors and actions all the way to the broader community they live in and its associated public health issues. Although rates of violence in society, overall, have decreased, violence in schools has been on the rise. Schools have been bombarded with an inordinate amount of violent threats and must ensure students stay safe by implementing safety protocols and procedures to assess and manage any threats of potential violence.

While social media has many inherent risks and can increase the rates of violence and bullying in schools, it can assist schools in communicating necessary information before, during, and after a crisis situation. Not only can harmful rumors and false information be rapidly dispelled, school leaders and even students can inform parents of important information in a timely manner.

Although it is easy to point to risk factors such as substance abuse or reasons such as a student's immediate environment as the cause of school violence, it is important that school authorities, teachers, counselors, parents, and students all understand that these variables are only a partial explanation. These influences on student behaviors such as bullying and other forms of violence are just that. Risk factors are only influences that make students more vulnerable to victimization and perpetration; they are not the direct cause of student violence.

POINTS TO REMEMBER

- *The presence of a threat does not guarantee violence just as the absence of a threat does not guarantee that nothing will occur.*
- *School leaders, law enforcement, and parents need to regularly engage with and understand relevant social media to understand students and their propensity for threatening or violent behavior.*
- *When conducting threat assessments, schools should focus on the perpetrator's motivation behind the threat, the credibility of the threat, if the perpetrator has the capability of, and tools to carry out the threat. In addition to the details and specificity of the threat, it is imperative that crisis teams focus on the behavioral actions related to the planning and carrying out of the threat.*
- *Social media, specifically text messages and cell phones, and the spreading of rumors has been found to create more anxiety among students than actual threats or incidents that may have triggered the rumors in the first place.*
- *Increased access to guns, coupled with prior victimization, including bullying and cyberbullying, places students at a heightened level of vulnerability for committing acts of gun violence and carrying guns to school.*

Chapter 5

Protocols that Protect

Successful Systems to Ensure School Safety

Today's schools are susceptible to numerous hazards and threats that can immediately turn into emergency situations with life-threatening consequences. As such, it is necessary that schools have emergency procedures and protocols in place to take quick and decisive action in a crisis situation that will keep students safe (Graves, 2017).

There are a multitude of practices and procedures that schools use, such as locking and monitoring doors, to promote the safety of students, faculty, and staff. Measures such as these, along with the use of metal detectors and security cameras, seek to limit or control access to school buildings and restrict students' and visitors' behavior on school grounds (National Center for Education Statistics, 2018).

A series of statistics from the 2015 to 2016 academic year shows the measures many schools have gone to in order to keep students safe.

- 94 percent of public schools reported that they controlled access to school buildings by locking or monitoring doors during school hours;
- 81 percent of schools used security cameras to monitor the school;
- 68 percent required faculty and staff to wear badges or picture IDs;
- 53 percent enforced a strict dress code;
- 25 percent of schools used random dog sniffs to check for drugs;
- 21 percent required students wear uniforms;
- 7 percent required students to wear badges or picture IDs; and
- 4 percent used random metal detector checks (National Center for Education Statistics, 2018).

The use of a variety of safety and security procedures also differed by school level and school size during the 2015–16 school year. More public primary schools and public middle schools controlled access to school buildings and required faculty and staff to wear picture IDs than public high schools (National Center for Education Statistics, 2018). Public schools with an enrollment of 1,000 or more students reported using security cameras, student IDs, random dog sniffs, and random metal detector checks than schools with fewer enrolled students (National Center for Education Statistics, 2018). These safety and security measures were also more prevalent in schools where 76 percent or more of the students were eligible for free or reduced-price lunch than in schools where a lower percentage were eligible (National Center for Education Statistics, 2018).

During 2015–16, 94 percent of public schools had a plan and protocols in place in the event of a bomb threat and 92 percent of schools had protocols in place in the event of a school shooting (National Center for Education Statistics, 2018). Similarly, 95 percent of schools drilled students on lockdown procedures, 92 percent drilled students on evacuation procedures, and 76 percent drilled students on shelter-in-place procedures (National Center for Education Statistics, 2018).

Despite concrete security measures, research suggests that in order to make schools safer, administrators should focus on the softer human side of school security, such as building relationships with students, improved counseling and mental health support, regular planning and cross-training with first responders, diversified lockdown and evacuation drills, and a proactive communications strategy with parents and the community (Finkel, 2017).

SCHOOL EMERGENCY PLANNING

To assist schools in school emergency planning and security, Homeland Security and Emergency Management (2014) created a school guide to provide schools with examples, tools, procedures, resources, and guidance when planning for emergencies.

Authorities and Responsibilities

Local school districts have the authority to develop plans for school emergencies and crises as well as the responsibility to coordinate with other agencies in the development of necessary standards for local school system emergency plans (Homeland Security and Emergency Management, 2014).

Superintendents and other administrative staff have the obligation to recommend school safety, violence prevention programs, and emergency preparedness programs to the local school board in addition to assigning teaching staff to participate in the District Response Team (Homeland

Security and Emergency Management, 2014). Emergency coordinators should be appointed to help with planning, monitoring, and implementation of an emergency plan, including in-service exercises, drills, and trainings for all school personnel (US Department of Education, Office of Elementary and Secondary Education, Office of Safe and Healthy Students, 2013).

School administrators are also required to initiate, administer, participate, and evaluate school safety and emergency programs to ensure a coordinated response for all schools in the district. Once local policies, needs, and experiences have been evaluated, school administrators are also responsible for implementing any necessary changes to their school emergency plans (Homeland Security and Emergency Management, 2014).

Principals have the authority to act as the school emergency coordinator and assign specific staff to be a part of the Building Response Team, assign the selected staff school emergency responsibilities, and monitor the staff's participation in any designated training and competencies (US Department of Education, Office of Elementary and Secondary Education, Office of Safe and Healthy Students, 2013).

Principals may also encourage the incorporation of school safety, violence prevention, and emergency preparedness into teachers' curricula (Homeland Security and Emergency Management, 2014). By incorporating school safety into the classroom, teachers can help students develop confidence in their ability to care for themselves and help others, particularly in emergency situations (Homeland Security and Emergency Management, 2014).

Teachers should also participate in developing school emergency plans and participate in the execution of emergency plan exercises, drills, and trainings. They can also provide valuable instruction and practice in universal emergency response procedures (US Department of Education, Office of Elementary and Secondary Education, Office of Safe and Healthy Students, 2013).

Students not only have an obligation to cooperate during emergency drills and exercises, they are also responsible for themselves and others in an actual emergency situation. It is vital that students understand the importance of reporting situations of concern and take an active part in school emergency preparation, planning, and response (Homeland Security and Emergency Management, 2014).

EMERGENCY MANAGEMENT: PREVENTION/MITIGATION

School districts can take action to minimize the impact and/or reduce the probability of school violence and emergency situations by examining all potential hazards to avoid or lessen their impact (US Department of Education, Office of Elementary and Secondary Education, Office of Safe and Healthy Students, 2013). School policies and curricula that address facilities, school security, and the school culture/climate should also be assessed to create a safe, healthy, orderly, and supportive school environment (Homeland Security and Emergency Management, 2014).

Many schools already have curricula and programs that aim to prevent students from engaging in harmful behaviors, including social problem-solving programs, anti-bullying programs, and school-wide discipline efforts. In addition to these, schools should, if they have not done so already, implement threat assessment procedures that will identify students, or even staff, who may pose a threat to themselves or others (Homeland Security and Emergency Management, 2014).

Safe School Assessments

In planning and preparing for school emergencies, it is essential that schools implement a process to assess the school for safety and identify their strengths, risks, and areas of weakness (US Department of Education, Office of Elementary and Secondary Education, Office of Safe and Healthy Students, 2013). Assessments can help ensure that schools have a welcoming, healthy, physical environment and identify any hazards or obstructions that could impede an effective response to violence (Homeland Security and Emergency Management, 2014).

School assessments can bring school and community stakeholders and response agencies together to create an environment where students feel safe (Homeland Security and Emergency Management, 2014). The assessment process should include a review of any existing school emergency plans and procedures followed by a discussion and evaluation of not only those emergency plans and procedures, but staff training exercises and any other items that cannot be physically observed during a walk-through of the school's interior and exterior (US Department of Education, Office of Elementary and Secondary Education, Office of Safe and Healthy Students, 2013).

Once the review is complete, the assessment team should generate a report and provide recommendations for improvement. Documentation on successful prevention efforts and existing resources should be included in the report along with the potential risks and areas of weakness identified during the assessment (Homeland Security and Emergency Management, 2014). This will allow administrators to prioritize solutions and proceed with a plan for addressing the most pressing school safety concerns (Homeland Security and Emergency Management, 2014).

Threat Assessment

Threat assessments serve to prevent targeted violence and by having a threat assessment process, schools are able to build violence-reduction strategies that can create healthy cultures of safety, respect, and emotional support for students and staff (Homeland Security and Emergency Management, 2014). Threat assessment processes are generally most effective when they are included in bigger violence prevention strategies and when policies and programs are developed and implemented using a multidisciplinary approach (Cornell, 2018).

The first step in conducting a threat assessment is to identify students of concern who pose a threat and may have the capacity and capability to actually commit an act of violence (Homeland Security and Emergency Management, 2014). Once any students have been identified, the threat assessment team should work to gather and examine any information and evidence of behaviors or conditions that indicate the student(s) may be planning or preparing for an attack (Cornell, 2018).

Information that may provide insight into a student's situation, motives, intentions, and risk for potential violence can be gleaned from not only student records but interviews with staff, students, parents, potential targets, and the student(s) of concern (Homeland Security and Emergency Management, 2014). Interviews should focus on facts and behaviors rather than the assessment team's interpretations of the behaviors or comments (Cornell, 2018). Any data gathered should also be corroborated through multiple sources (Cornell, 2018).

When all relevant information has been gathered and analyzed, the threat assessment team should be able to determine the credibility of the threat. If the team deems a threat incredible, the student of concern may still need additional assistance or support and the team's priority should then be to make the appropriate referrals to prevent any future acts of violence (Homeland Security and Emergency Management, 2014).

EMERGENCY MANAGEMENT: PREPAREDNESS

Emergency preparedness is a coordinated effort between local school districts, individual schools, and the community at large to develop a school emergency plan and decide what actions will be taken and who will respond in an emergency situation (US Department of Education, Office of Elementary and Secondary Education, Office of Safe and Healthy Students, 2013). As part of the preparation process, school emergency response teams should be structured around key management roles. The team should designate an individual to be in command who will then have the overall responsibility for managing the incident and have the direct responsibility for disseminating public information and liaising with community response agencies (Homeland Security and Emergency Management, 2014).

Another individual will be in charge of operations and be responsible for responding to the incident by directing actions, developing objectives, and organizing and directing resources (US Department of Education, Office of Elementary and Secondary Education, Office of Safe and Healthy Students, 2013). Another team member should be responsible for logistics and be instilled with the responsibility of identifying and providing the necessary resources and services to support any incident response needs (Homeland Security and Emergency Management, 2014).

Other team members may also be assigned to the planning and financial phases in which they would develop action plans, collect and evaluate information, identify issues, make recommendations for future actions, and manage any financial aspects of an incident such as costs, recordkeeping, and insurance (US Department of Education, Office of Elementary and Secondary Education, Office of Safe and Healthy Students, 2013).

Drills

Drills are a crucial component of emergency planning and preparedness and provide schools with the opportunity to reveal weaknesses in procedures, improve response and coordination, clarify roles and responsibilities, and improve individual performances (Homeland Security and Emergency Management, 2014). Drills not only demonstrate a school's commitment to prepare for emergencies, they also test universal procedures such as lockdowns, evacuations, and shelters-in-place, build staff and student awareness, and provide training to students and staff (Cornell, 2018).

At the beginning of each school year, schools should create a drill schedule that varies the time of the drill, such as during lunch periods or class changes, changes the evacuation routes that are available to students, and/or places a fake hazardous material component to each fire drill (Homeland Security and Emergency Management, 2014; Finkel, 2017). This provides students and staff with simulated emergencies that administration can use to better understand how to react should it ever be necessary.

EMERGENCY MANAGEMENT: RESPONSE

Response is the process of implementing appropriate actions while an emergency situation is in process. During this phase of emergency management, schools and districts mobilize any resources and implement any universal emergency procedures, such as lockdown, shelter-in-place, reverse evacuation, evacuation/relocation, and reunification, that are necessary to manage the emergency (Homeland Security and Emergency Management, 2014).

Lockdown

Although lockdowns are utilized during active shooter incidents, they are more likely to be used for hazards and threats such as a missing student, medical emergencies, aggressive people in or near the school, bomb threats, threats of shooting, or gunshots heard near the school (Granite School District, 2016; Graves, 2017). On a national level, there is no standardized terminology for school lockdowns and school districts may choose a terminology that includes numeric designations such as "Level 1, 2, and 3 Lockdown" or terminology that uses color designations such as "Code Yellow and Code Red Lockdown," or other terms such as "Shelter-in-Place, Lock in, or Lock out" (Graves, 2017).

When there is a threat to student safety on campus, schools may be placed in a lockdown, requiring all students, staff, and approved visitors to secure themselves in a room away from immediate danger (Granite School District, 2016). Although classroom activities may be allowed to continue during a lockdown, locked doors cannot be opened by anyone except emergency personnel who must first announce and identify themselves before unlocking the door from the outside (Graves, 2017).

During situations where there is a direct threat to student safety, such as a dangerous person on or near the school, a credible or time-sensitive threat, an act of violence such as a shooting, stabbing, or hostage situation, or a fatality, a lockdown with cover may be initiated (Graves, 2017). During this type of lockdown, all students, staff, and visitors move to the nearest room, lock the door, turn off the lights, and stop all classroom activities. Students and staff should also take cover in an area of the room that is the least visible from the door and exterior windows and remain absolutely quiet, making the room look and sound unoccupied (Granite School District, 2016; Graves, 2017).

In situations such as medical emergencies, school administrators may declare a lockdown but allow movement in one part of school and set another part off limits. In this instance, the goal is to provide privacy for the student, reduce trauma among bystanders, and clear the way for first responders (Graves, 2016). During lockdowns, schools should ensure that all cell phone communications cease and communication using the school's phone system and social media accounts is used to provide accurate and timely updates on any emergency situation that is occurring (Granite School District, 2016; Homeland Security and Emergency Management, 2014).

Shelter-in-Place

A shelter-in-place is initiated by local law enforcement or school administration when there is a potential threat to student safety off school grounds, such as in a nearby neighborhood. During a shelter-in-place, students and staff are to remain in the building, or brought inside if outside the building, with all exterior doors locked and continue school activities as normal inside the school (Granite School District, 2016). During this time, the front door of the school is managed by a school administrator or police officer and, unless otherwise directed, parents and visitors are not allowed on school grounds until the protocol has ended. If the shelter-in-place extends beyond the end of the school day, parents should receive communication from the school regarding pickup accommodations and any disrupted bus schedules (Homeland Security and Emergency Management, 2014).

Reverse Evacuation

Reverse evacuation procedures are implemented when conditions inside the building are safer than those outside the building and can be used in combination with other procedures such as lockdowns and shelters-in-place to ensure the safety of students and staff who are outside the building (Homeland Security and Management, 2014).

Evacuation/Relocation

Evacuation procedures are used when conditions are safer outside the building than inside the building and evacuation routes should be specified according to the type of emergency. For example, when a bomb threat has occurred, building administrators should determine the safest evacuation route based on the known or suspected location of the device (US Department of Education, Office of Elementary and Secondary Education, Office of Safe and Healthy Students, 2013).

When planning primary and secondary relocation sites, administrators should consider distance, accessibility, hours of operation, transportation, and amenities as well as reach agreements with owners of non-district buildings that can be used for relocation/reunification sites (Homeland Security and Emergency Management, 2014).

Student Reunification/Release

Reunification planning involves identifying available staff, particularly those without classroom duties, to lead the reunification process. It is important that staff be trained on reunification procedures and schools should consider using tabletop exercises to test procedures and identify potential gaps or complications (Homeland Security and Emergency Management, 2014). The most crucial aspect of reunification is matching the right child with the right parent and to ensure a smooth reunification process, schools must have the most current emergency contact information (US Department of Education, Office of Elementary and Secondary Education, Office of Safe and Healthy Students, 2013).

Successful reunification also requires coordination and cooperation between schools and community emergency response agencies. Clear expectations and a clear understanding of school and community roles should be established. For example, it should be made clear what specific aspects of the reunification process schools will manage, and that other roles, such as traffic control, crowd control, or medical assistance, will be provided by emergency responders (Homeland Security and Emergency Management, 2014).

EMERGENCY MANAGEMENT: RECOVERY

The goal of recovery is to restore the learning environment and infrastructure of the school back to normal as quickly as possible. When planning for recovery, which takes place in the preparedness phase, the four main components of emotional, academic, physical/structural, and business/fiscal must be addressed (Homeland Security and Emergency Management, 2014). The recovery process may be short term or long term depending on the circumstances of the event, the amount of time necessary, and the allocation of resources (US Department of Education, Office of Elementary and Secondary Education, Office of Safe and Healthy Students, 2013).

Emotional recovery assists students, families, staff, and administrators with the physical, psychological, and/or emotional trauma that can occur as a result of experiencing a tragic event. Schools should provide training to any staff member that wishes to facilitate the healing process by assisting with the emotional impact of an event and help students and other staff return to the normal routine of school (Miller, 2014). In turn, designated building and grounds personnel should work with the school district and insurance company during the physical/structural recovery process to ensure the safety and usability of a building after a crisis event (Homeland Security and Emergency Management, 2014).

The critical business functions of a school must be restored as soon as possible, including payroll systems, accounting, and access to personnel and student data (Homeland Security and Emergency Management, 2014). During this fiscal recovery phase, it is also important that schools have a continuity of

operations plan to ensure there is a smooth transition of authority and responsibility in the event that lead administrators are unable to perform their duties
and responsibilities as a result of a crisis or traumatic incident (US Department of Education, Office of Elementary and Secondary Education, Office of
Safe and Healthy Students, 2013).

Academic recovery must occur and seek to restore the structure and routine
of learning to enhance and support the healing process. Schools need to be
mindful that changes in routine may occur and with the collaboration of staff,
students, and families, a "new normal" will be reached (Homeland Security
and Emergency Management, 2014).

To help students recover, classes should be resumed as soon as possible
and changes to the academic routine may be made if any of the school facilities have been significantly damaged and cannot be used safely (Homeland
Security and Emergency Management, 2014). Home instruction or tutoring
may be a viable option for those students that are unable to attend school
and the rescheduling of assignments and exams will aid in instances of lost
instruction time and unavailable teaching materials (Homeland Security and
Emergency Management, 2014).

There should also be regular communication with all staff, whether it be
in person, via email, or in printed form, regarding any modifications and to
provide information on resources such as counseling (Homeland Security and
Emergency Management, 2014).

Following a crisis or traumatic event, it is essential that coping and resil-
iency be promoted as part of a school's social/emotional recovery. Research
demonstrates that after a crisis, both children and adults demonstrate a wide
range of reactions including physical, cognitive, and emotional symptoms
(Homeland Security and Emergency Management, 2014). Schools must
recognize that for some, any adverse effects may lessen with emotional support as time goes on, but others may experience longer-term consequences.
In either situation, these emotional reactions are very normal responses to
very abnormal events (US Department of Education, Office of Elementary
and Secondary Education, Office of Safe and Healthy Students, 2013).

FINAL THOUGHTS

Although schools are susceptible to a variety of hazardous and threatening
situations that can turn into a life-threatening emergency on a moment's
notice, there are procedures and protocols that can be implemented not only
to mitigate a school's risk, but to assist them in taking a quick and decisive
action in a crisis situation. Practices and procedures such as locked, monitored doors, metal detectors, security cameras, lockdowns, and shelters in

place all promote and seek to ensure the safety of administrators, teachers, staff, students, and visitors.

Preparing for emergencies and keeping students safe must be a coordinated effort between local school districts, individual schools, and the larger community. Processes such as school safety assessments, threat assessments, and drills will all serve to identify a school's strengths, risks, and weaknesses and ensure that schools remain a welcoming, healthy, and safe physical environment for students and staff.

POINTS TO REMEMBER

- *Concrete security measures, meaningful relationships with students, counseling and mental health support, planning and cross-training with first responders, lockdown and evacuation drills, and proactive communications strategies, used together, will ensure that students remain safe in school.*
- *Schools can mitigate their risk of becoming a victim of school violence and other crisis situations by continuously assessing their policies and curricula that address facilities, school security, and school culture/climate to ensure the school maintains a safe, healthy, orderly, and supportive environment.*
- *It is essential that students understand their role in keeping schools safe and the importance of reporting any issues of concern as well as their responsibility to keep themselves and others safe by taking an active part in school emergency preparation, planning, and response.*
- *When conducting a threat assessment, it is imperative that team members focus on facts and behaviors that can be corroborated rather than rely on their impressions and interpretations of a student's concerning behavior. Although a threat may not be deemed credible, it is important to remember that students may still need referrals to supportive resources.*

Chapter 6

All Are Invited

Addressing the Needs of Marginalized Student Populations

Schools across the country welcome and serve students from diverse backgrounds; yet many report feeling targeted and unsafe (Loschert, 2016). From 1999 to 2014, the percentage of schools controlling or limiting access to their buildings increased from 75 percent to 93 percent, security camera usage increased from 19 percent to 75 percent, and law enforcement officers were present in 43 percent of public schools (NASP, 2017a; Loschert, 2016).

Students, school administrators, and teachers agree that school violence represents a real threat to school safety and can deprive students and teachers of a safe and productive learning environment (Constitutional Right Foundation, 2018). Students that are victims of school violence can experience symptoms of extreme stress, adversity, and trauma that can impede their concentration, cognitive functioning, memory, and social relationships (Miller, 2014). Signs of extreme of stress can be evidenced by external symptoms such as reactivity, aggression, and misbehavior, and internal symptoms such as hypervigilance, anxiety, depression, grief, fear, anger, and isolation (de Albuquerque & Williams, 2015).

The chronic and significant stress placed on victimized students increases their risk for developing other mental health issues, all undermining their ability to effectively function while at school (de Albuquerque & Williams, 2015). As a result, teachers might notice an increase in student absences, distracted behaviors, withdrawal, irritability, and other noticeable changes in students who may feel that they have been targeted (NASP, 2017c).

Those students that are more at risk for being a victim of school violence include students that are disabled, from disadvantaged backgrounds, from ethnic, racial, linguistic, cultural, or religious minorities, and/or perceived as having a sexual orientation or gender identity different from what is considered normal (NASP, 2017c). These groups of students are all faced with stigmatization, discrimination, and exclusion and, as a result, are more likely to be bullied both in person and online (United Nations General Assembly, 2016; NASP, 2017c).

MINORITY STUDENTS

Historically, underserved students have been more likely to witness and experience violent acts and face a greater risk of exposure to violence and, most recently, African American and Latino students report being even more afraid of becoming a victim of school violence (Loschert, 2017). Over the last ten years, although the rate of violent incidents in public schools has declined from thirty-one incidents to an estimated eighteen incidents per 1,000 students, the majority of them can still be found in schools that predominantly serve students of color (Loschert, 2017). More specifically, schools that have a minority population of 50 percent or more reported twenty-one violent incidents per 1,000 students in 2015–2016 as compared to forty incidents per 1,000 students for schools with less than a 50 percent minority population during the same time period (Loschert, 2017).

To further combat school violence, educators have been implementing formal programs specifically designed to prevent or reduce school-based violence that range from teaching specific curricula on topics such as conflict resolution, anti-bullying, anger management, and counseling, and psychological support (Loschert, 2017; Fronius et al., 2016). These programs have been most prevalent in schools that have a large minority population with 42 percent of schools engaging in restorative discipline practices that focus on repairing the harm caused by school violence and preventing future incidents by building positive relationships (Loschert, 2017; Ortega et al., 2016). In comparison, only 15 percent of schools that serve the highest percentage of white students use these same approaches (Loschert, 2017; Ortega et al., 2016).

Research has consistently shown that programs and policies within a school that emphasize prevention, student support, and a positive school climate can reduce misbehavior and incidents of violence (Watchel, 2016). Efforts that help students feel safe, engaged, connected, and supported create a positive school climate in which students can flourish academically by improving their grades, having a strong attendance record, forming positive relationships with peers and adults, and minimizing risky behavior (Loschert, 2017; Fronius et al., 2016).

SOCIALLY AND ECONOMICALLY
DISADVANTAGED STUDENTS

Meta-research from twenty-eight studies over the last forty-five years on three different continents indicates that there is actually a tenuous connection between socioeconomic status and being a bully (Tippett & Wolke, 2014). Results actually indicated that bullies exist across all socioeconomic groups and are as likely to be found in deprived inner city areas as they are in suburban schools in well-to-do neighborhoods (Tippett & Wolke, 2014).

Students from low socioeconomic status families do have an increased risk of being victimized at school, particularly if they stand out from their peer group for not being able to afford the same level of lifestyle (Tippett & Wolke, 2014). Although victims of bullying, particularly those who unsuccessfully retaliate, are more likely to live in lower socioeconomic status families, socioeconomic status is not the most accurate indicator to identify which students will become involved in school bullying (Rivara & Le Menestrel, 2016; Tippett & Wolke, 2014).

When trying to determine which students may become bullies and which students will become their victims, it is important to examine a combination of background and family factors that differ based on socioeconomic level, such as parenting or sibling relationships, parenting strategies, and individual characteristics (Rivara & Le Menestrel, 2016). Those students who have overprotective, helicopter parents, are subject to harsh parenting practices, and are exposed to high rates of domestic violence, are all at an increased risk of becoming a victim of bullying (Tippett & Wolke, 2014).

Bullies can be found as a part of each social strata and social conditions, especially those in hierarchical school settings, and not just socioeconomic status; any student is at risk of becoming a victim of school violence and bullying (Rivara & Le Menestrel, 2016). Students who are socially and economically disadvantaged and are faced with discrimination, humiliation, and bullying while at school, may experience feelings of powerlessness and may be unable to speak out about school violence issues fearing they will not be believed, or worse, blamed for the violent incidents themselves (United Nations General Assembly, 2016).

LGBTQ+ STUDENTS

Homophobic bullying can take many forms such as cyberbullying, verbal bullying, social exclusion, as well as physical and psychological violence and runs rampant throughout school systems across the world (UNESCO, 2017; United Nations General Assembly, 2016). Students who identify as one of the many designations under the LGBTQ+ umbrella are more likely to experience violence at school, creating an inescapable continuum of threatening experiences that leaves them feeling isolated, unsafe, and worthless, in addition to putting them at risk for dropping out of school (Rivara & Menestrel, 2016; Loschert, 2016).

A recent study of close to 2,500 educators and students across the United States found that the adults were less comfortable intervening with bullying due to sexual orientation and gender identity than when bullying behavior was based on race, ability, and religion (Minero, 2018). Of the educators surveyed, 83 percent believed they should provide a safe environment for their LGBTQ+ students by displaying visible symbols of support and disciplining students for using homophobic language; yet, only half of them had done so (Minero, 2018).

This lack of support stems from teachers feeling uncomfortable talking to students about sexuality due to personal beliefs or perceptions about what is considered appropriate or from administrative and/or parental pressures not to talk about it (Minero, 2018). Making it all the more difficult, teachers undergo little, if any, professional development on how to address LGBTQ+ issues and bullying, establish LGBTQ+ inclusive cultures, or identify anti-LGBTQ+ behaviors and harassment (Minero, 2018). To compound the difficulty in having constructive dialogue, the allowance of transgender students to use bathrooms aligned with their identity has raised the LGBTQ+ profile across the nation (Minero, 2018).

This lack of support from school can have a substantial impact on students. Research shows that lesbian, gay, and bisexual students are two to three times more likely to be bullied as non-LGBTQ+ peers, more likely to miss school, and five times as likely to attempt suicide, with transgender students at an even higher risk of suicide (Minero, 2018). Moreover, another study found that lesbian, gay, and bisexual students that were victims of bullying reported higher levels of substance abuse and risky behaviors than their heterosexual peers who were bullied (Minero, 2018).

STUDENTS WITH DISABILITIES

Students with disabilities are faced with many daily obstacles including managing their physical, emotional, mental, or learning disabilities while simultaneously trying to overcome the same academic challenges that all students face (Chen, 2017). Research indicates that students with disabilities also have to contend with the challenge that they are more likely than their non-disabled peers to be targets of school violence, often perpetrated by their teachers

(Chen, 2017). One Chicago study found that while students with disabilities made up only 16 percent of the city's overall public school population, they accounted for 24 percent of school gun violence victims (Chen, 2017).

Coupled with these challenges are the difficulties students with disabilities face with the implementation of safety measures schools are taking in the wake of school violence. Lockdowns and evacuation drills are now occurring on a regular basis and, as a result, students with disabilities encounter disruptions to their routine, unrealistic behavior expectations, accessibility problems, and other challenges that may not be addressed in an Individualized Education Plan (IEP) (Embury & Clarke, 2018).

In order to comply with a drill or actual crisis, students with disabilities are expected to maintain silence, follow directions very quickly, maintain a position or location, manage feelings of stress, and manage changes to their schedule (Embury & Clarke, 2018; Clarke, Embury, Jones, & Yssel, 2014). In order to help students with disabilities in crisis situations, schools should start by evaluating the overall safety plan and create individualized plans for students with disabilities that include key personnel who provide regular support and are familiar with the students (Exceptional Child, 2018; Clarke et al., 2014).

Although most schools have crisis plans to support student safety, few of these plans address the complex needs of students with disabilities; thus, personalized plans will help students progress in the attainment of these skills by integrating them into their learning process (Clarks et al., 2014). As a result, students will be more prepared in the event of a lockdown or emergency during school (Embury & Clarke, 2018).

INDIVIDUALIZED EMERGENCY AND LOCKDOWN PLANS

Embury and Clarke (2018) recommend that schools develop an individualized emergency learning plan (IELP) for students who have significant health, behavioral, and/or communication needs, require significant physical supports, or require support for activities of daily living. When creating IELPs, teachers and school administrators should consider the diverse range of intellectual, social, emotional, and physical development of students with disabilities and allow for adequate practice opportunities and teachers to have necessary medical supplies and equipment on hand for emergency situations (Clarke et al., 2014).

IELPs allow teachers to write down what accommodations each student will need and share specific concerns related to how a student follows directions and responds to emergency situations (Clarke et al., 2014). When appropriate, teachers should consult with students about needed supports in a time of crisis or emergency and to ensure that self-advocacy skills can be used to share their needs with support personnel (Clarke et al., 2014).

When developing IELPs, issues of confidentiality should be addressed. Schools may consider sharing information with first responders and/or any individual involved in supporting the student in response to a crisis. Schools may also add a waiver for parents to sign that would give the school permission to share critical student information with appropriate crisis response personnel (Clarke et al., 2014).

All crisis plans should also take into consideration travel problems that may be common for students with disabilities, particularly those that use wheelchairs or crutches or for those who have an impaired gait (Clarke et al., 2014). An example might be a student who needs to be transferred onto a blanket or other carrying device to get through blocked hallways due to a fire or natural disaster.

Ideally, students with disabilities should carry their IELP, whether it be in their daily organizer, iPad, or in their backpack, along with any necessary medication or communication devices. Similarly, teachers should keep copies of students' IELPs in a variety of locations where it will be easily accessible to school administrators, school and emergency personnel, and the students' parents (Clarke et al., 2014).

Of critical importance, is the ability of students with disabilities to communicate with emergency personnel and differentiate between helpful adults and those who want to do harm (Clarke et al., 2014). Students should be taught to recognize features of emergency personnel, such as badges, uniforms, hats, and jackets to assist them in identification as well as given opportunities to see and practice talking with emergency personnel in nonemergency situations (Clarke et al., 2014).

THE CALL FOR ACTION

Recently, governments around the world adopted the first ever call for action document on homophobic violence in education that provided for an inclusive and equitable education for all learners in an environment that is free from discrimination and violence (United Nations General Assembly, 2016). This document recognized that any form of school violence interferes with students' rights to equal access to education and educational opportunities for all students and that countries cannot achieve this if there are students being discriminated against or experiencing violence because of their actual or perceived sexual orientation and gender identity/expression (United Nations General Assembly, 2016).

Cross-cultural efforts are now focused on comprehensive approaches that promote inclusion and diversity, address and prevent violence, and consider the legal and sociocultural contexts across the globe (Wells, Fox, & Cordova-Cobo, 2016). Strategic actions include monitoring the prevalence of school violence, establishing comprehensive national and school-level policies, training for teachers and school staff, and evaluating the efficiency, effectiveness and impact of responses to violence (Wells et al., 2016).

Trauma-Sensitive Approaches and Interventions

One way to comprehensively approach the ramifications of school violence among students is to create schools that specialize in trauma by equipping existing schools with the staff and resources necessary to provide trauma-sensitive responses and supports (Cole, Eisner, Gregory, & Ristuccia, 2013; Dwyer, O'Keefe, Scott, & Wilson, 2012). In these schools, student behavior is viewed as a potential outcome of life circumstances rather than willful disobedience or intentional misbehavior (NASP, 2017c).

Through training, teachers will be able to understand the impact of trauma on school functioning and be able to see their students' behavior through this lens. As a result, relationships of trust will be built, students will be able to develop the skills needed to self-regulate behaviors, emotions, and attention, and student success and overall health and well-being will be supported (Cole et al., 2013; Dwyer et al., 2012).

Schools across the world share the responsibility to identify students that may be at an increased risk of victimization. Comprehensive approaches and multitiered systems of support that are focused on educational, social, emotional, and behavioral outcomes are more effective than clinical approaches and often prevent the need for intensive, direct services (Cole et al., 2013). Forming school-based teams, along with parental and student referral mechanisms, can help determine which students may require more intensive crisis intervention and/or counseling services (NASP, 2017c).

To promote student well-being and a sense of belonging, schools should focus on students' strengths, including each individual's unique skills and knowledge, by building upon them and creating opportunities for students who are comfortable to share their knowledge and ideas and be heard (Cole et al., 2013). Grouping motivated students, teachers, and/or school resource officers with students who are feeling alienated to work on service-learning projects can lead to shared goals, objectives, and activities that can counteract the emotional effects of school violence (Constitutional Rights Foundation, 2018).

Research indicates that those students most at risk for delinquency and violence are often those who are most alienated from the school community (Council for Exceptional Children and Council for Children with Behavioral

Disorders, 2013). Addressing the underlying problems that lead to school violence and building positive connection between students provides a platform for all students to engage in cooperative learning and develop new and useful skills, attitudes, and behavior as well as model new behaviors and form positive role models (Cole et al., 2013; Dwyer et al., 2012). Allowing students to participate in the planning and implementation of service-learning projects will likely lead them to buy into activities that demonstrate value and relevance as well as increase feelings of connectedness to the education and school (Constitutional Rights Foundation, 2018).

FINAL THOUGHTS

Students, staff, and families around the globe all agree that violence is a real threat to school safety. Violence has the potential to deprive students not only of their right to an equal education, but a safe and productive learning environment as well. With the recent call to action and the adoption of the first document on homophobic violence, governments around the world are taking a stand to reduce violence and increase student safety.

Students that identify as LBGTQ+ are at an increased risk of victimization and, as a result, likely to drop out of school. Disadvantaged students feel powerless and blamed. Students with disabilities encounter the trials and tribulations of life with a disability and the added challenges of achieving an education. All marginalized groups have the potential to feel victimized not only by their peers, but the adults that are supposed to protect and teach them.

Although research indicates schools are becoming safer, the need for a comprehensive approach to supporting the victims of school violence is growing. Trauma-sensitive schools can provide students with the staff and support they need in times of crises. Through training, teachers and administrators will better understand the emotional outcomes of school violence for both victims and perpetrators and have a better ability to work with students on developing the skills necessary to attain academic success and overall health.

POINTS TO REMEMBER

• *Students most at risk for being victimized by school violence include those students that are disabled, from disadvantaged backgrounds, from ethnic, racial, linguistic, cultural, or religious minorities, and/or perceived as having a sexual orientation or gender identity different from what is considered normal.*

- *Although schools make plans for crisis and emergency situations, very few schools have implemented safety plans that address the complex needs of students with disabilities. To ensure the safety of these students, schools should create personalized plans, particularly for students who have significant health, behavioral, and/or communication needs, require significant physical supports, or require support for activities of daily living.*
- *Any form of school violence interferes with students' rights to a free and safe education and their rights to be free from violence.*

Chapter 7

Strong Partners in Prevention

School-Community-Police Relations

According to the National Center for Education Statistics, there are approximately 46,000 full-time and 36,000 part-time school resource officers in the United States charged with the critical responsibility of keeping students safe during school (Tomar, 2018; Devlin & Gottfredson, 2018). Urban communities that are filled with crime, poverty, drugs, and gang violence increase the safety risks for public school education and confirm the need for police presence (Tomar, 2018).

With 65 percent of schools still reporting incidents of serious violent crimes, including weapons use, threats, robberies, and sexual assaults, law enforcement agencies play a vital role in school safety; yet, this is not their problem alone (Schweit & Mancik, 2017; Wood, 2018). Improved school security should be a collaborative effort between students, schools, parents, the wider community, and local law enforcement and when implemented properly, functions as a defense against criminal behavior and acts as a bridge between law enforcement and the community (Wood, 2018; Tomar, 2018).

RELATIONSHIPS WITH SCHOOLS

Due to the diverse nature and varying needs of schools, a needs assessment should be conducted to determine school goals and the involvement, if any, of law enforcement (Schweit & Mancik; Federal Bureau of Investigation, 2017). Minimally, schools should have a relationship with local law enforcement and a contact in the police department (Schweit & Mancik, 2017; Federal Bureau of Investigation, 2017).

In order to assist schools in determining the type of school-police partnership that will be most effective in their community and ensure safe, school-based enforcement through collaboration, understanding, and respect, the US Departments of Education (DOE) and Justice (DOJ) have designed the SECURe Local Implementation Rubric (US Department of Education and US Department of Justice, 2016).

Before being assigned to a school, officers should receive three levels of specialized training before they are qualified for the unique challenges of working within a school (Schweit & Mancik 2017; Tomar, 2018). At a minimum, training should clearly set forth the role of the officer within the school, provide avenues for de-escalation and diversionary tactics in place of demanded compliance, assist officers in the recognition of students with disabilities, and provide instruction on how to work with this population's unique and variable needs (Tomar, 2018; US Department of Education and US Department of Justice, 2016).

Ideally, training should also include current laws applicable to the educational environment. Of critical importance are state and federal laws regarding privacy and juveniles, search and seizure, and information sharing (Schweit & Mancik, 2017; US Department of Education and US Department of Justice, 2016). At the same time, it is essential that all officials, law enforcement officers and agencies, and emergency personnel have crisis intervention and de-escalation training (Schweit & Mancik, 2017).

Working with students presents unique challenges due to various developmental and legal considerations. Specialized training should also be considered in recognizing signs of trauma, abuse, and exposure to violence, cultural sensitivity and competency, linguistic differences, adolescent development, school discipline and codes of conduct, and positive behavior management (Federal Bureau of Investigation, 2017; Tomar, 2018; US Department of Education and US Department of Justice, 2016).

MEMORANDUM OF UNDERSTANDING

With law enforcement's increased role in the daily routines of local schools, questions have arisen on whether students' misconduct is the responsibility of law enforcement rather than the school (Klein, 2016; Canady, James, & Nease, 2012). In order to formalize roles and responsibilities, clarify expectations, and address concerns before they develop, schools and law enforcement officials enter into written agreements known as a memorandum of understanding, or MOU (U.S. Department of Justice: Office of Community Oriented Policing Services, 2014).

MOUs focus on two categories of law enforcement officers who interact with students on school campuses (Klein, 2016). Both municipal police officers and school police officers are trained, and certified peace officers authorized to carry a firearm and make arrests (Klein, 2016). Municipal police officers are local, uniformed police officers employed by the local police department who are assigned to patrol in and around a school campus while school police officers are employees of a school district police agency (Klein, 2016). One of the advantages of having a school police department with officers that are technically school officials is flexibility and fewer barriers between school, police, health, and welfare data sharing (Canady et al., 2012).

MOUs clearly outline officer roles and responsibilities and can help preserve the use of police time and resources for safety-related issues and leave the responsibility for disciplinary issues with the school. This delineation also helps reduce unnecessary student involvement with the juvenile justice system as well as unintended disproportionate minority contact (Klein, 2016; Canady et al., 2012).

Goals and themes that should be addressed in an MOU include the improvement and maintenance of school safety, promotion of student and staff positive experiences with law enforcement, protection of students' privacy and dignity, reduction of police involvement for minor offenses, and reduction of disparities for students of color and other vulnerable populations (Klein, 2016).

MOUs can also describe additional roles that school officers may be assigned or undertake in school settings such as involvement in activities that support a safe learning environment, build positive relationships with students, and avoid the criminalization of students for minor misconduct (Canady et al., 2012). An example of such a situation is a school resource officer who is paired with an at-risk student to provide mentorship and guidance (Klein, 2016).

MOUs should be evaluated on a regular basis and revised using input from school administrators, local law enforcement, students, parents, and other stakeholders to reflect changes in local needs and concerns (US Department of Education and US Department of Justice, 2016).These agreements should also be shared with other schools in the community for feedback and information on best practices as well as with state and local officials to inform policy related to officers in schools (US Department of Education and US Department of Justice, 2016).

LEGAL ISSUES

Search and Seizure

MOUs ensure that students suspected of wrongdoing are advised of their rights in a clear and understandable manner before being interviewed by a law enforcement official. It is essential in an MOU to specifically clarify whose responsibility it is to conduct searches and seizures within a school as school administrators have a much lower standard of reasonable suspicion to conduct searches of students, backpacks, lockers, and/or student cars parked on campus (Klein, 2016).

Parental Notification and Consent

MOUs provide the protection of student victim or witness rights by providing for parental notification and consent as well as Miranda warning procedures so that no harm will come to a victim or witness who later becomes a suspect (US Department of Justice: Office of Community Oriented Policing Services, 2014). Parental notification requires the school administrator to make immediate contact with a parent regarding where the student is being taken. Parental consent must be obtained before any interrogation of a minor occurs and in cases where the parent wishes to be present, students are not made available for questioning until the parent is present (Klein, 2016; Canady et al., 2012).

Student Privacy

There are a multitude of federal and state laws and regulations that limit information sharing between agencies. The federal Family Educational Rights and Privacy Act (FERPA) prevents law enforcement agencies from obtaining a student's education information without a prior agreed-upon process to ensure privacy, while the Federal Health Insurance Portability and Accountability Act (HIPPA) creates barriers to sharing health care information between agencies (Klein, 2016). Confidentiality must also be maintained in accordance with all other applicable federal and state regulations although barriers to sharing student data with school police officers are less as the officers are employed by the school and act as school officials (Klein, 2016).

Data Collection and Reporting

Processes for appropriate data collection, analysis, and reporting are often outlined in MOUs not only for partnership evaluation purposes but to evaluate the extent to which school policies and police officer actions may be disproportionately impacting students of color, those with special needs, or other affected youth (US Department of Education and US Department of Justice, 2016).

Data can be used to address disproportionate minority contact with police and the juvenile justice system and potentially reduce the rate of school-based arrests while maintaining a safe school climate (Klein, 2016). Policy revision may become necessary if data indicate that a school-based law enforcement program is being conducted inconsistently with federal and state constitutions, civil rights laws, and applicable privacy laws (US Department of Education and US Department of Justice, 2016).

RESOURCE OFFICERS: ROLES, RESPONSIBILITIES, AND RELATIONSHIPS

To ensure partnership effectiveness, school resource officers should plan formal assessment time to conduct school climate surveys to examine the relationship with the school and assess strengths, identify areas that need improvement, and monitor progress toward the stated goals (US Department of Education and US Department of Justice, 2016). Continuous assessment also allows school crime statistics and related changes to be tracked over time and in the aftermath of incidents of targeted school violence, reevaluate the school's current crisis plan (Federal Bureau of Investigation, 2017).

Crucial to successful partnerships between schools and law enforcement, consistent and clear communication should occur and allows both parties to address any needs and problems in the partnership as they arise (Federal bureau of Investigation, 2017). At a minimum, meetings should be scheduled monthly to ensure effective communication and include details about who can access digital codes and security-related equipment as well as initiate critical incident responses (Schweit & Mancik, 2017).

If conflict should arise and school officers face resistance from school personnel, parents, or the broader community, a comprehensive approach to school safety should be reinforced. MOUs between schools and local law enforcement should specify any applicable guidelines, authoritative roles, and methods for conflict resolution (US Department of Justice: Office of Community Oriented Policing Services, 2014). Distinctions should also be made on how disciplinary versus criminal actions should be handled while avoiding harsh disciplinary policies when possible (Federal Bureau of Investigation, 2017).

Relationship Building

To establish trustworthy relationships, school officers may address students by name, greet them and ask about their day, show genuine concern and interest in their lives, and consistently ensure communications remain respectful (Schweit & Mancik, 2017; Federal Bureau of Investigation, 2017). Officers must recognize students' developmental maturity, cultural or linguistic differences, and consider any potential prior trauma or previous involvement with law enforcement in order to gain trust (Schweit & Mancik, 2017).

Research shows that in 81 percent of school attacks, there was at least one other student who knew of the impending attack on the school (Volungis & Goodman, 2017). When students trust school officials, they are more likely to report the potential behavior (Schweit & Mancik, 2017). Strong relationships and connections between school officers and students are essential to building a healthy school climate where communication is encouraged, and student feels safe in raising awareness of potential threats to school safety (Schweit & Mancik, 2017; Canady et al., 2012).

Research has also shown that students will not report a threat or suspicious behavior if they are in fear of negative repercussions, doubt the validity of the threat, do not know who to advise, or think they have more time to react (Schweit & Mancik, 2017). One of the most important things a school officer can do is remind students that what they do matters and can actually save lives (Federal Bureau of Investigation, 2017).

To break down barriers, officers can relate success stories from their community, educate students on how they may report potential safety issues, and reassure students on confidentiality (Schweit & Mancik, 2017). Of critical importance, the overall safety of schools and the rarity of violence, particularly targeted incidents, must be emphasized (Devlin & Gottfredson, 2018). Using specific, age-appropriate examples, officers can express the ways in which students can contribute to and ensure school safety (Schweit & Mancik, 2017).

School officers should avoid arresting students or bringing criminal charges against a student when more metered responses are available (Schweit & Mancik, 2017). Aggressive tactics for minor infractions can strain school officer-student relationship and will negatively impact school climate, discourage students from reporting potentially suspicious or harmful behavior, and disproportionately introduce youth into the criminal justice system (Devlin & Gottfredson, 2018).

School Climate and the Resource Officer

In addition to their regular law enforcement duties, school officers should help to foster a healthy school climate that allows students to feel safe and supported, especially when reporting threats and suspicious behavior (Schweit & Mancik, 2017). Officers are in a position, through honest discussions with students, to change the perception of school safety and police and emphasize the students' role and responsibility in promoting and supporting a healthy school climate (Schweit & Mancik, 2017; Devlin & Gottfredson, 2018).

School officers are also in a unique position to promote respectful communication and encourage students to use nonviolent ways of resolving conflict. Officers can teach students that violence is not an appropriate response to conflict and provide education on nonviolent conflict resolution strategies such as peer mediation and active listening (Federal Bureau of Investigation, 2017).

The presence of an officer within a school system can help deter crime or de-escalate a violent situation, particularly when officers visit classrooms and lunchrooms and provide supervision in places where students are likely to congregate (Schweit & Mancik, 2017; Devlin & Gottfredson, 2018). Officers can also participate in or attend more collective school-based activities, such as music, theater, sports, language festivals, clubs, and activities. These small group events can assist officers in building trustworthy connections and provide improved opportunities to integrate themselves as an intimate part of the educational environment (US Department of Education and US Department of Justice, 2016).

School resource officers should interact with students and the wider school community during times of training, particularly those that discuss bullying and prevention strategies. Officers should actively participate in trainings to become familiar with state bullying laws and adequate prevention methods as well as participate in the school's anti-bullying program (Federal Bureau of Investigation, 2017).

School campus safety-related training can also be provided to students to ensure that they know how to react during potentially dangerous or threatening situations. Officers can run training programs for active shooter incidents, internet safety, and learning the distinction between snitching, tattling, and telling (Federal Bureau of Investigation, 2017).

SCHOOL TO PRISON PIPELINE

With police officer presence in schools up from 10 percent in 1997 to 30 percent in 2014, there has been conflicting research about whether schools are safer from school violence and/or the likelihood of a school shooting (Klein, 2018; Devlin & Gottfredson, 2018). One recent study found that 53 percent of the population believe that police officers make schools safer while the remaining 47 percent believe that police do not belong in public schools (Tomar, 2018).

Some research has found that the presence of police in school programs is beneficial where the focus is on student safety and education (McLachlan, 2018; Devlin & Gottfredson, 2018). Police presence can result in timely information sharing between agencies, effective child protection and welfare responses, and engagement in school-based restorative justice and anti-bully-ing processes (McLachlan, 2018).

Other research found that the presence of armed police officers and zero tolerance policies in schools can potentially change the environment from one that supports student academic and social development to one that is under constant surveillance and where adults expect the worst of students (McLachlan, 2018; Cole, 2017). Having police in school may increase the possibility for police brutality as there were at least 87 incidents of school police using stun guns on kids for a range of behaviors between 2011 and 2016 (Klein 2018).

Students who would not otherwise come to the attention of the criminal justice system may now be identified as criminals for low-level offenses and funneled into the criminal justice system (McLachlan, 2018; Klein, 2018; Cole, 2017). This school-to-prison pipeline disproportionately pushes students of color, those who identify as LGBTQ+, have disabilities, and/or are English language learners, out of school and into the prison system for minor school infractions and disciplinary matters (Klein, 2018; Elias, 2013; National Education Association, 2016; Cole, 2017).

Students with disabilities, for example, account for 25 percent of those who were arrested in schools and 75 percent of them have been physically restrained on school grounds (Tomar, 2018; Elias, 2013; Cole, 2017). Of students that comprise the ethnic minority, 70 percent of Black and Latino students faced referral to law enforcement or school-related arrests (Tomar, 2018; Elias, 2013; Cole, 2017).

The ability of school officers to effectively keep children safe has been undermined by evidence of excessive police force, racial bias, and the rein-forcement of the school-to-prison pipeline (Tomar, 2018). Tension between school officers and students is on the rise and confrontations between law-enforcement and unarmed, underaged students, even for minor offenses, are becoming heated (Tomar, 2018).

On a more systemic level, the line between disciplinary and criminal matters is quite blurry. With a reported 70 percent of school officers being involved in routine disciplinary matters and the rise in zero-tolerance disci-plinary policies where school administrators are not allowed to use discretion or change punishments to fit individual circumstances, more students than ever before are finding themselves in the courthouse instead of the principal's office (Tomar, 2018; National Education Association, 2016; Cole, 2017; Devlin and Gottfredson 2018).

Students in schools with police presence are five times more likely to be arrested than students in schools without a police presence (Tomar, 2018). During the 2011–2012 school year, there were 260,000 students referred to law enforcement and 92,000 students were subjected to school-based arrests

(Tomar, 2018). For these students, their educational opportunities are diminished, and they become much more likely to drop out of school, struggle for employment, and spend their lives in and out of jail (National Education Association, 2016; Cole, 2017; Devlin & Gottfredson, 2018).

Diverting the School-to-Prison Pipeline

School districts have the power to divert students away from the school-to-prison pipeline. Schools should compile annual reports on the total number of disciplinary actions that have pushed students out of the classroom based on gender, race, and ability (Elias, 2013). Entering into MOUs with law enforcement and school officers should help limit arrests at schools and reduce the use of force by law enforcement (Elias, 2013). Detailed explanations of infractions and the approved responses should also be set out in the school's code of conduct to ensure fairness (Elias, 2013).

Teachers should be trained on, and increase their use of, restorative justice practices, trauma-based resources, and positive behavioral interventions and supports, particularly for at-risk students (Elias, 2013). Students whose behavioral issues stemmed from the presence of disabilities, for example, may benefit from more specialized instruction within the school rather than criminal prosecution (Tomar, 2018). For those students whose difficulties arose from family problems, community support resources would have been more helpful, and for students whose behavioral difficulties originated with mental health or substance abuse issues, counseling and intervention would have been beneficial (Tomar, 2018; Devlin & Gottfredson, 2018).

Treating students as criminals for acting out in minor, nonviolent ways not only weakens the authority of educators and police, it suggests that those in positions of authority are not trustworthy, fair, and are even immoral (Cole, 2017). Schools may inadvertently teach students that school administrators, teachers, and law enforcement cannot be respected or trusted, thus fostering conflict between them and students, which, in turn, then leads students to experience further exclusionary and damaging punishment (Cole, 2017).

AFTER SCHOOL PROGRAMS

Another way in which schools, communities, and students can build relationships of trust and understanding with law enforcement, is by police-afterschool program partnerships (Silverberg, 2017). The more time the officers can spend with students, the stronger their relationships will become (Mitchell, 2015). These programs not only provide a safe space for students to focus on academics outside of school, they also keep kids off the street and away from neighborhood crime (Charles Stewart Mott Foundation, 2016).

The New York Sheriffs Institute, for example, runs a six-week summer camp each year with 140 new students each week that focuses on topics from bullying to internet safety (Murphy, 2016a). The New York police are also involved in community-based organizations and centers such as the Boys and Girls Club and the Department of Parks and Recreation (Silverberg, 2017). Programs include "Hoops with Heroes" where teens are able to teach local officers about basketball and, in turn, officers teach participants about the value of teamwork and sportsmanship (Murphy, 2016b). California takes athletics one step further and extends into academics as the Police Athletic and Activity League provides students with assistance on homework, creative writing and reading time, and enrichment activities such as educational games, athletics, and outdoor activities (Murphy, 2016b).

FINAL THOUGHTS

Thousands of full-time and part-time school resource officers in the nation's school systems have been charged with the indispensable responsibility of keeping children safe while at school, even in the most unforgiving neighborhoods of poverty, crime, and drugs. As such, it is critical that MOUs exist between school administration and local law enforcement that delineate the officers' roles and responsibilities, particularly when it comes to issues of discipline. The goal of police presence within schools is ultimately to keep everyone safe and any unnecessary student involvement with the juvenile justice system and unintended disproportionate minority contact should be kept to a minimum.

To ensure safety, school resource officers serve as a trusted mentor and advisor, particularly for at-risk students. Strong, trusting relationships and connections between school officers and students must be established to maintain a healthy school climate where there is open and honest communication and students feel safe in raising awareness of potential threats to school safety. Through straightforward and honest discussion, officers and students, together, can take responsibility in changing the perception of school safety and promoting and supporting a healthy school climate overall.

Through school officers, students can be shown that there are alternative ways to solve conflict in lieu of violence. Students can be trained in nonviolent conflict resolution strategies as well as shown how to promote respectful communication. These skills, in addition to other positive behavioral interventions such as special education, counseling, and community resource outreach, can then help divert students away from the school-to-prison pipeline, keeping more students in school and increasing rates of student success.

POINTS TO REMEMBER

- *It is essential that school administrations and local law enforcement enter into a Memorandum of Understanding (MOU) to clearly define roles and responsibilities, particularly for issues of misconduct, and address the legal rights of students, such as proper search and seizure, parental consent and Miranda rights, FERPA, and HIPPA, before any issues arise.*
- *The school-to-prison pipeline introduces students to the criminal justice system who would not otherwise be categorized as criminals and disproportionately pushes students of color and other protected statuses out of school and into the juvenile justice system. In addition, zero-tolerance policies in schools take away the school's administrative power to use discretion and change punishment to fit with individual circumstances.*
- *Although police presence in schools is continually undermined by evidence of excessive police force, racial bias, and the existence of the school-to-prison pipeline, schools are safe and violence and targeted incidents within schools are rare.*
- *Students benefit from positive interactions with school resource officers and those who participate in afterschool and summer programs.*

References

Agrawal, A.J. (2017). What role is media playing in school shootings? Retrieved from https://www.huffingtonpost.com/aj-agrawal/what-role-is-social-media_b_9033612.html.

Ahmed, S., & Walker, C. (2018). School shootings so far in 2018. Retrieved from https://www.cnn.com/2018/03/02/us/school-shootings-2018-list-trnd/index.html.

Allan, A., & Madden, M. (2008). *Hazing in View: College Students at Risk: Initial Findings from the National Study of Student Hazing.* Retrieved from https://ocm.auburn.edu/stop_hazing/National_Hazing_Study.pdf.

American Academy of Child and Adolescent Psychiatry. (2017). *Bullying Resource Center.* Retrieved from https://www.aacap.org/aacap/Families_and_Youth/Resource_Centers/Bullying_Resource_Center/Home.aspx.

American Psychological Association [APA]. (2018). *School Connectedness.* Retrieved from http://www.apa.org/pi/lgbt/programs/safe-supportive/school-connectedness/default.aspx.

Andone, D. (2017). *Finland Found a Proven Way to Combat Bullying. Here's What it'll Take to Make it Work in the US.* Retrieved from https://www.cnn.com/2017/08/11/health/finland-us-bullying-prevention-trnd/index.html.

Associated Press. (1996). $900,000 won by gay man in abuse case. *The New York Times.* Retrieved from https://www.nytimes.com/1996/11/21/us/900000-won-by-gay-man-in-abuse-case.html.

Asher, J. (2015). *Making the Case for Social Media in Schools.* Retrieved from https://www.edutopia.org/blog/making-case-social-media-in-schools-jim-asher.

Australia. (2017). *Enhancing Online Safety for Children Amendment Act 2017.* Retrieved from https://www.ilo.org/dyn/natlex/docs/ELECTRONIC/105254/128682/F-237304532/AUS105254.pdf.

Batsche, G.M., & Knoff, H.M. (1994). Bullies and their victims: Understanding a pervasive problem in the schools. *School Psychology Review, 23*(2), 165–175. Retrieved from https://eric.ed.gov/?id=EJ490574.

Bauer, G.F. (2017). The application of salutogenesis in everyday settings. In M. Mittlemark et al., *The Handbook of Salutogenesis*, 153–158. DOI: 10.1007?978-3-319-04600-6_16.

Bazelon, E. (2010). *Was Phoebe Prince Once a Bully?* Retrieved from http://www .slate.com/articles/life/bulle/2010/08/was_phoebe_prince_once_a_bully.html.

Bazelon, E. (2014). *Sticks and Stones: Defeating the Culture of Bullying and Rediscovering the Power of Character and Empathy.* New York: Random House.

Benbenishty, R., Astor, R.A., Roziner, I., & Wrabel, S.L. (2016). Testing the causal links between school climate, school violence, and school academic performance: A cross-lagged panel autoregressive model. *Education Researcher, 45*(3), 197–206. DOI: 10.3102/0013189X16644603.

Billings, S.B., Deming, D.J., & Rockoff, J.E. (2012). *School Segregation, Educational Attainment and Crime: Evidence from the End of Busing in Charlotte-Mecklenburg.* Retrieved from https://www0.gsb.columbia.edu/faculty/jrockoff/pap ers/w18487.pdf.

BLIA. (2015). *#PurpleMySchool Campaign Making Education Safer for LGBTI Students.* Retrieved from https://medium.com/being-lgbti-in-asia/purplemyschool-campaign-making-education-safer-for-lgbti-students-9060a05413f4.

Bloch, A.M. (1977). The battered teacher. *Today's Education, 66*(2), 58–62. Retrieved from https://eric.ed.gov/?id=EJ182374.

Bowes, L., Arsenault, L., Maughan, B., Taylor, A., Caspi, A., & Moffitt, T.E. (2009). School, neighborhood, and family factors are associated with children's bullying involvement: A nationally representative longitudinal study. *Journal of American Academy Child Adolescent Psychiatry, 48*(5), 545–553. DOI: 10.1097/ CHI.0b013e31819cb017.

Canady, M., James, B., & Nease, J. (2012). To protect and educate: The school resource officer and the prevention of violence in schools. *National Association of School Resource Officers.* Retrieved from https://nasro.org/cms/wp-content/up loads/2013/11/NASRO-To-Protect-and-Educate-nosecurity.pdf.

Carter, B.B., & Spencer, V.G. (2006). The fear factor: Bullying and students with disabilities. *International Journal of Special Education, 21*(1), 11–23.

Centers for Disease Control and Prevention. (2016). *Understanding School Violence.* Retrieved from https://www.cdc.gov/violenceprevention/pdf/school_violence_f act_sheet-a.pdf.

Centifanti, L.C.M., Fanit, K.A., Thomson, N.D., Demetriou, V., & Anastassiou-Hadjicharalambous. (2015). Types of relational aggression in girls are differentiated by callous-unemotional traits, peers and parental control. *Behavioral Sciences, 5*(4), 518–536. DOI: 10.3390/bs5040518.

Centre for Educational Research and training and DevTech Systems, Inc. (2008). *The Safe Schools Program: A Qualitative Study to Examine School-related Gender-based Violence in Malawi.* Retrieved from http://www.ungei.org/srgbv/files/Sa fe_Schools_Malawi_PLA_Report_January_8_2008.pdf.

Charles Stewart Mott Foundation. (2016). *Partnerships between Police and Afterschool Programs Build Relationships, Break Down Barriers.* Retrieved from https://www.mott.org/news/articles/police-officers-dedication-afterschool-leads-local-state-national-partnerships/.

Chen, G. (2017). How to protect special education students from school violence. Retrieved from https://www.publicschoolreview.com/blog/how-to-protect-speci al-education-students-from-campus-violence.

Clarke, L.S., Embury, D.C., Jones, R.E., & Yssel, N. (2014). Supporting students with disabilities during school crises: A teacher's guide. *TEACHING Exceptional Children, 46*(6), 169–178.

Cohen, J., & Freiberg, J.A. (2013). School climate and bullying prevention. *National School Climate Center*. Retrieved from https://www.schoolclimate.org/themes/sch oolclimate/assets/pdf/practice/sc-brief-bully-prevention.pdf.

Cohn, A., & Canter, A. (2003). *Bullying: Facts for Schools and Parents*. Retrieved from http://www.naspcenter.org/factsheets/bullying_fs.html.

Cole, N.L. (2017). Understanding the school-to-prison pipeline: Definition, empirical evidence, and consequences. Retrieved from https://www.thoughtco.com/school-to -prison-pipeline-4136170.

Cole, S.F., Eisner, A., Gregory, M., & Ristuccia, J. (2012). *Creating and Advocating for Trauma-sensitive Schools*. Retrieved from https://traumasensitiveschools.org/ wp-content/uploads/2013/11/HTCL-Vol-2-Creating-and-Advocating-for-TSS.pdf.

Constitutional Rights Foundation. (2018). School violence prevention strategy. Retrieved from http://www.crf-usa.org/school-violence/school-violence-preve ntion-strategy.html.

Cornell, D. (2018). *Threat Assessments Crucial to Prevent School Shootings*. Retrieved from https://www.huffingtonpost.com/entry/threat-assessments-crucial-t o-prevent-school-shootings_us_5abd0af7e4b075a5c9a465f7.

Cornell, D.G., & Limber, S.P. (2016). Do U.S. laws go far enough to prevent bullying at school? *American Psychological Association, 47*(2), 64. Retrieved from http:// www.apa.org/monitor/2016/02/ce-corner.aspx.

Council for Exceptional Children and Council for Children with Behavioral Disorders. (2013). Protecting students and teachers: A discussion on school safety. Retrieved from http://cecblog.typepad.com/files/protecting-students-and-teachers -hearing-testimony-final-5.pdf.

Cox, J.W., & Rich, S. (2018). *Scarred by School Shootings*. Retrieved from https ://www.washingtonpost.com/graphics/2018/local/us-school-shootings-history/? utm_term=.1c64a7f6805b#about.

Crews, G.A., & Counts, M.R. (1997). *The Evolution of School Disturbance in America*. Westport, CT: Praeger Publishers.

Cullen, D. (2009). *Columbine*. New York, NY: Hatchette Book Group.

Dastagir, A.E. (2018). Are Boys 'Broken'? Another Mass Shooting Renews Debate on Toxic Masculinity. *USA Today*. Retrieved from https://www.usatoday.com/ story/news/2018/02/19/boys-broken-another-mass-shooting-renews-debate-toxic -masculinity/351125002/.

Dawkins, J.L. (1996). Bullying, physical disability and the paediatric patient. *Developmental Medical Child Neurology, 38*(7), 603–612. DOI: 10.1111/j.1469- 8749.1996.tb12125.x.

de Albuquerque, P.P., & Williams, L.C.A. (2015). Impact of the worst school experiences in students: A retrospective study on trauma. *Paideia, 25*(62), 343–351. DOI: 10.1590/1982-43272562201508.

Del Giudice, V. (2018). *U.S. Mass Shootings from 1949 to 2018: Summary of Incidents*. Retrieved from https://www.bloomberg.com/news/articles/2018-06-28/u-s-mass-shootings-from-1949-to-2018-summary-of-incidents.

Devlin, D.M., & Gottfredson, D.C. (2018). The roles of police officers in schools: Effects on the recording and reporting of crime. *Youth Violence and Juvenile Justice, 16*(2), 208–223.

Diliberti, M., Jackson, M., & Kemp, J. (2017). Crime, violence, discipline, and safety in U.S. public schools: Findings from the school survey on crime and safety: 2015–16 (NCES 2017–122). *U.S. Department of Education, National Center for Education Statistics*. Retrieved from https://nces.ed.gov/pubs2017/2017122.pdf.

Disini Law Office. (2015). *RA 10627: The Anti-Bullying Act*. Retrieved from https://elegal.ph/republic-act-no-10627-the-anti-bullying-act/.

Dupuy, B. (2017). Mother attacks Pittsburg teacher with brick over a school phone ban: Police. Retrieved from http://www.newsweek.com/teacher-attacked-taking-students-cell-phone-689492.

eNCA. (2016). *Norway Tried to Improve Statistics on Bullying in Schools*. Retrieved from https://www.enca.com/world/norway-tries-to-improve-statistics-on-bullying-in-schools.

Enyinnaya, E. (2018). Violence in schools: Causes and solutions. Retrieved from http://www.voicesofyouth.org/en/posts/violence-in-schools--2.

Espelage, D. (n.d.). *Preventing Bullying and Violence*. Retrieved from https://www.futureswithoutviolence.org/preventing-bullying-and-violence/.

Espelage, D., Anderman, E.M., Brown, V.E., Martinez, A., Lane, K., McMahon, S.D., … Reynolds, C.R. (2013). Understanding and preventing violence directed against teachers. *American Psychologist, 68*(2), 75–87. DOI: 10.1037/a0031307.

Evans, R., & Thompson, M.G. (2016). Parents who bully school. *National Association of Independent Schools*. Retrieved from https://www.nais.org/magazine/independent-school/spring-2016/parents-who-bully-school/.

Floyd, N.M. (1985). "Pick on somebody your own size?": Controlling victimization. *The Pointer, 29*(2), 9–17. DOI: 10.1080/05544246.1985.9944687.

Finley, T. (2013). *In their Own Words: Teachers Bullied by Colleagues*. Retrieved from https://www.edutopia.org/blog/teachers-bullied-by-colleagues-1-todd-finley.

Finkel, E. (2017). Nailing down the right lockdown procedure for school security. Retrieved from https://www.securitymagazine.com/articles/88533-nailing-down-the-right-lockdown-procedure-for-school-security.

Fisman, R. (2013). *Brown v Board Reduced Crime*. Retrieved from http://www.slate.com/articles/business/the_dismal_science/2013/04/desegregation_and_crime_resegregation_has_led_to_a_spike_in_violent_crime.html.

Florida, R., & Boone, A. (2018). *Where do Mass Shootings Take Place*. Retrieved from https://www.citylab.com/life/2018/03/where-do-mass-shootings-take-place/554555/.

Fronius, T., Persson, H., Guckenburg, S., Hurley, N., & Petrosino, A. (2016). Restorative justice in U.A. schools: A research review. Retrieved from https://jprc.wested.org/wp-content/uploads/2016/02/RJ_Literature-Review_20160217.pdf.

Fukkink, R.G., Bruns, S., & Ligtvoet, R. (2016). *Voices of Children from Around the Globe: An International Analysis of Children's Issues at Child Helplines.* DOI: 10.1111/chso.12150.

Gershoff, E.T. (2016). School corporal punishment in global perspective: Prevalence, outcomes, and efforts at intervention. *Psychology, Health & Medicine, 22*(1), 224–239. DOI: 10.1080/13548506.2016.1271955.

Gibson, N., & O'Gorman, K. (2017). *Blurred Lines: Building Winning Athletes in Sport or Just Plain Bullying?* Retrieved from https://theconversation.com/blurred -lines-building-winning-athletes-in-sport-or-just-plain-bullying-74001.

Gladden, R.M., Vivolo-Kantor, A.M., Hamburger, M.E., & Lumpkin, C.D. (2014). Bullying surveillance among youths: Uniform definitions for public health and recommended data elements, version 1.0. *National Center for Injury Prevention and Control, Centers for Disease Control and Prevention and U.S. Department of Education.* Retrieved from https://www.cdc.gov/violenceprevention/pdf/bullyin g-definitions-final-a.pdf.

Gordon, C. (2014). *By the Numbers: Sexual Violence in High School.* Retrieved from http://america.aljazeera.com/watch/shows/america-tonight/articles/2014/11/14/by- the-numbers-sexualviolenceinhighschool.html.

Gordon, S. (2018). *How Educators can Support Victims of Bullying.* Retrieved from https://www.verywellfamily.com/how-educators-can-support-victims-of-bullyin g-460719.

Granite School District. (2016). *School Safety Protocols Explained in Graphics.* Retrieved from https://www.graniteschools.org/blog/2016/08/16/granite-schoo l-district-will-begin-using-these-security-terms/.

Graves, S.M. (2017). *Lockdown Terminology in K-12 Schools: Why it is ok to Use Codes and Which Codes are Best.* Retrieved from https://www.hsdl.org/?abstract &did=798734.

Greenbaum, S. (1987). What can we do about schoolyard bullying? *Principal, 67*(2), 21–24. Retrieved from https://eric.ed.gov/?id=EJ363350.

Greene, R.W. (2015). *Collaborative & Proactive Solutions: A Crucial Treatment Approach in Trauma Sensitive Schools.* Retrieved from https://www.attachme nttraumanetwork.org/wp-content/uploads/Collaborative-Problem-Solving-Dec-20 15.pdf.

Gubar, J. *Fanaticus: Mischief and Madness in the Modern Sports Fan.* Lanham, MD: Roman & Littlefield.

Guryan, J. (2004). Desegregation and black dropout rates. *American Economic Review, 94*(4), 919–943. DOI: 10.3386/w8345.

Hazelden Foundation. (2016). *Violence Prevention Works! Safe Schools, Safer Com- munities.* Retrieved from http://www.violencepreventionworks.org/public/olwe us_bullying_prevention_program.page.

Hill, C., & Kearl, H. (2011). Crossing the Line: Sexual Harassment at School. *Ameri- can Association of University Women.* Retrieved from https://www.aauw.org/file s/2013/02/Crossing-the-Line-Sexual-Harassment-at-School.pdf.

Hoffman, J. (2010). Online bullies pull schools into the fray. *The New York Times.* Retrieved from https://www.nytimes.com/2010/06/28/style/28bully.html.

Homeland Security and Emergency Management. (2014). Comprehensive school safety guide. Retrieved from https://www.nfpa.org/-/media/Files/Public-Educatio n/By-topic/Schools/MinnesotaSchool-Safety-Guide.ashx?la=en.

Horton, P. (2018). The bullied boy: Masculinity, embodiment, and the gendered social-ecology of Vietnamese school bullying. *Gender and Education, 30*(5). DOI: 10.1080/09540253.2018.1458076.

Hyman, I.A., & Perone, D.C. (1998). The other side of school violence: Educator policies and practices that may contribute to student misbehavior. *Journal of School Psychology, 36*(1), 7–27. DOI: PII S0022-4405(97)000047-2.

Hyman, I.A., & Wise, J.H. (1979). *Corporal Punishment in American Education.* Philadelphia, PA: Temple University Press.

Johnson, R.C. (2011). *Long-run Impacts of School Desegregation and School Quality.* DIO: 10.3386/w16664.

Kimmel, M. (2014). *Assault on Gay America.* Retrieved from https://www.pbs.org/ wgbh/pages/frontline/shows/assault/interviews/kimmel.html.

Klein, J. (2012). *The Bully Society: School Shootings and the Crisis of Bullying in America's Schools.* New York University Press.

Klein, M. (2016). *Keys Elements of Memoranda of Understanding that Formalize School-police Partnerships: Analysis of Four Recent Agreements in California.* Retrieved from https://strongnation.s3.amazonaws.com/documen ts/116/98d41307-1265-4fd4-8f04-1ca7a1051403.pdf?1473683596&inline; %20filename=%22MOU-Formalizing%20School-Police%20Partnerships_FC_ CA.pdf%22.

Kosciw, J.G., Greytak, E.A., Giga, N.M., Villenas, C., & Danischewski, D.J. (2015). *The 2015 National School Climate Survey: The Experiences of Lesbian, Gay, Bisexual, Transgender, and Queer Youth in Our Nation's Schools.* Retrieved from https://www.glsen.org/article/2015-national-school-climate-survey.

Kosciw, J.G., Greytak, E.A., Palmer, N.A., & Boesen, M.A. (2013). *The 2013 National School Climate Survey: The Experiences of Lesbian, Gay, Bisexual, and Transgender Youth in Our Nation's Schools.* Retrieved from https://www.glsen.or g/sites/default/files/2013%20National%20School%20Climate%20Survey%20Fu ll%20Report_0.pdf.

Lambert, R. (2013). *Violence in U.S. K-12 schools, 1974–2013: Patterns in deadly incidents and mass threat.* Washington, DC: The Rural School and Community Trust.

Lang, N. (2018). New study: Rates of anti-LGBTQ school bullying at 'unprecedented high'. Retrieved from https://www.thedailybeast.com/new-study-rates-of-anti-l gbtq-school-bullying-at-unprecedented-high.

Langman, P. (2009). *Why Kids Kill: Inside the Minds of School Shooters.* New York, NY: St. Martin's Griffin.

Li, K. (2013). *In Kenya, a Child Helpline Proves a Lifeline for a Young Victim of Rape, and her Family.* Retrieved from https://www.unicef.org/protection/kenya_ 70988.html.

Lindert, J. (2017). Cyberbullying and its impact on mental health. *European Journal of Public Health, 27*(3). DOI: 10.1093/eurpub/ckx187-581.

Logue, J.M. (2008). Violent death in American schools in the 21st century: Reflections following the 2006 Amish school shootings. Retrieved from http://www15.uta.fi/arkisto/aktk/projects/sta/Logue_2008_Violent-Death.pdf.

Loschert, K. (2016). *The Suspension Effect: Exclusionary Discipline Practices Increase High School Dropout Rates and Cost the Nation Billions in Lost Tax Revenue, according to the Center for Civil Rights Remedies.* Retrieved from https://all4ed.org/articles/the-suspension-effect-exclusionary-discipline-practices-increase-high-school-dropout-rates-and-cost-the-nation-billions-in-lost-tax-revenue-according-to-the-center-for-civil-rights-remedies/.

Loschert, K. (2017). *Which Students are More Likely to be Victims of School Violence? New Report Provides Answers.* Retrieved from https://all4ed.org/which-students-are-more-likely-to-be-victims-of-school-violence-new-report-provides-answers/.

Lurie, J. (2014). Bullying victims are twice as likely to bring a weapon to school. Retrieved from https://www.motherjones.com/politics/2014/05/bullying-victims-carry-weapons-guns/.

Madigan, S., & Temple, J. (2018). 1in 7 teens are "sexting," says new research: Is consensual teen sexting a cause for concern? *Scientific American.* Retrieved from https://www.scientificamerican.com/article/1-in-7-teens-are-ldquo-sexting-rdquo-says-new-research/.

Mahnken, K. (2017). *The Hidden Mental Health Crisis in America's Schools: Millions of Kids not Receiving Services they Need.* Retrieved from https://www.realcleareducation.com/2017/11/08/the_hidden_mental_health_crisis_in_america039s_schools_45372.html.

Malekian, F., & Nordlof, K. (2012). *The Sovereignty of Children in Law.* Newcastle upon Tyne: UK.

Maynard, B.R., Vaughn, M.G., Salas-Wright, C.P., & Vaughn, S.R. (2016). Bullying victimization among school-aged immigrant youth in the United States. *Journal of Adolescent Health, 58*(3), 337–344. DOI: 10.1016/j.jadohealth.2015.11.013.

McCagny, C.H., Capron, T.A., Jamieson, J.D., & Carey, S.H. (2008). *Deviant Behavior: Crime, Conflict, and Interest Groups* (8th ed.). New York, NY: Routledge.

McKay, T., Misra, S., & Lindquist, C. (2017). Violence and LGBTQ+ communities: What do we know, and what do we need to know? *Violence and Victimization Research Program: Center for Justice, Safety and Resilience: RTI International.* Retrieved from https://www.rti.org/sites/default/files/rti_violence_and_lgbtq_communities.pdf.

McLachlan, K. (2018). *Police in Schools: Harmful or Helpful? It Depends on the Model.* Retrieved from https://theconversation.com/police-in-schools-helpful-or-harmful-it-depends-on-the-model-91836.

McLeod, S. (2017). *Behaviorist Approach.* Retrieved from https://www.simplypsychology.org/behaviorism.html.

McLeod, S. (2018). *Maslow's Hierarchy of Needs.* Retrieved from https://www.simplypsychology.org/maslow.html.

Merriam-Webster. (2018a). *Protocol.* Retrieved from https://www.merriam-webster.com/dictionary/protocol.

Merriam-Webster. (2018b). *Punishment.* Retrieved from https://www.merriam-webst er.com/dictionary/punishment.

Merton, R.K. (1938). Social structure and anomie. *American Sociological Review, 3*(5), 672–682. DOI: 10.2307/2084686.

Midlarsky, E., & Klain, H.M. (2005). A history of violence in the schools. In F. Denmark, H.H. Kraus, R.W. Wesner, E. Midlarsky, & U.P. Gielen eds., *Violence in Schools: Cross-national and Cross-cultural Perspectives.* DOI: 10.1007/0-387-28811-2.

Miller, A. (2014). Threat assessment in action. *American Psychological Association.* Retrieved from http://www.apa.org/monitor/2014/02/cover-threat.aspx.

Minero, E. (2018). *Schools Struggle to Support LBGTQ Students.* Retrieved from https://www.edutopia.org/article/schools-struggle-support-lgbtq-students.

Mitchell, C. (2015). *Programs Aim to Smooth Student-police Relations.* Retrieved from https://www.edweek.org/ew/articles/2015/05/20/program-aims-to-smooth-s tudent-police-relations.html.

Mitchell, K.J., Hamby, S.L., Turner, H.A., Shattuck, M.A., & Jones, L.M. (2015). Weapon involvement in the victimization of children. *American Academy of Pediatrics, 136*(1), 10–-17. DOI: 10.1542/peds.2014-3966.

Murphy, E. (2016a). Afterschool & law enforcement: Building relationships and trust. Retrieved from http://www.afterschoolalliance.org/afterschoolSnack/Aft erschool-Law-Enforcement-Building-relationships-and_08-02-2016.cfm.

Murphy, E. (2016b). Afterschool & law enforcement: Motivations for partnerships. Retrieved from http://www.afterschoolalliance.org/afterschoolSnack/Aftersch ool-and-law-enforcement-Motivations-for_07-07-2016.cfm.

Muschert, G.W., Henry, S., Bracy, N.L., & Peguero, A.A. (2014). *Responding to School Violence: Confronting the Columbine Effect.* Boulder, CO: Rienner Publishers.

NASP. (2016a). Social media and school crises. Retrieved from https://www.nasponli ne.org/resources-and-publications/resources/school-safety-and-crisis/social-medi a-and-school-crises.

NASP. (2016b). Using social media in crisis prevention and intervention. Retrieved from https://www.nasponline.org/resources-and--publications/resources/school-saf ety-and-crisis/social-media-and-school-crises/using-social-media-in-school-crisi s-prevention-and-intervention.

NASP. (2017a). Threat assessment for school administrators and crisis teams. Retrieved from https://www.nasponline.org/resources-and-publications/resources/ school-safety-and-crisis/threat-assessment-at-school/threat-assessment-for-school -administrators-and-crisis-teams.

NASP. (2017b). School violence prevention. Retrieved from https://www.nasponli ne.org/resources-and-publications/resources/school-safety-and-crisis/school-viol ence-prevention.

NASP. (2017c). School violence prevention: Guidelines for administrators and crisis teams. Retrieved from https://www.nasponline.org/resources-and-publications/r esources/school-safety-and-crisis/school-violence-prevention/school-violence-pre vention-guidelines-for-administrators-and-crisis-teams.

National Center for Education Statistics. (2018). *Indicator 20: Safety and Security Measures Taken by Public Schools.* Retrieved from https://nces.ed.gov/programs/crimeindicators/ind_20.asp.

National Education Association. (2016). Discipline and the school-to-prison pipeline (2016). Retrieved from https://ra.nea.org/business-item/2016-pol-e01-2/.

Netshitangani, T. (2014). Causes of school-based violence in South African public schools: Application of Normalisation Theory to understand the phenomenon through educators' perspectives. *Mediterranean Journal of Social Sciences, 5*(20), 1394–1402. DOI: 10.5901/mjss.2014.v5n20p1394.

Newman, K. (2004). *Rampage: The Social Roots of School Shootings.* New York, NY: Perseus Books.

Nijhara, K., Bhatia, S., & Unnikrishnan, B. (2018). Corporal punishment in children and its implications on mental health. *The Indian Journal of Pediatrics, 85*(5), 405. DOI: 10.1007/s12098-017-2525-8.

O'Brien, D. (2015). *New Zealand's Harmful Digital Communication Act: Harmful to Everyone Except Online Harassers.* Retrieved from https://www.eff.org/deeplinks/2015/07/nz-digital-communications-act-considered-very-harmful.

O'Keefe, G.S., & Clarke-Pearson, K. (2011). The impact of social media on children, adolescents, and families. *American Academy of Pediatrics, 127*(4). DOI: 10.1542/peds.2011-0054.

O'Keefe, J., Scott, P., & Wilson L. (2012). *Trauma and Young Children – A Caring Approach Project.* Retrieved from https://www.whealth.com.au/documents/work/trauma/LiteratureReview.pdf.

Olewus, D. (1978). *Aggression in the Schools: Bullies and Whipping Boys.* New York, NY: Wiley.

Olewus, D. (1991). Victimization among school children. In R. Baenninger ed., *Advances in Psychology, 76. Targets of Violence and Aggression,* 45–102. DOI: 10.1016/S0166-4115(08)61056-0.

Ophelia Project. (2012). *Relational Aggression Overview.* Retrieved from http://www.opheliaproject.org/ra.hmtl.

Ortega, L., Lyubansky, M., Nettles, S., & Espelage, D.L. (2016). Outcomes of a restorative circles program in a high school setting. *Psychology of Violence, 6*(3), 459–468. DOI: 10.1037/vio0000048.

PACER Center, Inc. (2016). *Bullying and Harassment of Students with Disabilities: Top 10 Facts Parents, Educators, and Students Need to Know.* Retrieved from http://www.pacer.org/publications/bullypdf/BP-18.pdf.

PACER Center. (2018). *Bullying Statistics.* Retrieved from http://www.pacer.org/bullying/resources/stats.asp.

Parkes, J., & Heslop, J. (2011). *Stop Violence against Girls in School: A Cross-country Analysis of Baseline Research from Ghana, Kenya, and Mozambique.* Retrieved from http://www.actionaid.org/sites/files/actionaid/svags_-_a_cross_country_analysis_of_baseline_research_from_ghana_kenya_and_mozambique.pdf.

Patchin, J.W., & Hinduja, S. (2016). 2016 Cyberbullying data. *Cyberbullying Research Center.* Retrieved from https://cyberbullying.org/2016-cyberbullying-data.

Payne, E., & Smith, E. (2013). LGBTQ kids, school safety, and missing the big picture: How the dominant bullying discourse prevents school professionals from thinking about systemic marginalization or…Why we need to rethink LGBTQ bullying. *QUE: A Journal in GLBTQ Worldmaking,* 1–36. DOI: 10.14321/qed.0001.

Perry, D.G., Kusel, S.J., & Perry, I.C. (1988). Victims of peer aggression. *Developmental Psychology, 24*(6), 807–814. DOI: 10.1037/0012-1649.24.6.807.

Petrosino, A., Guckenburg, S., DeVoe, J., & Hanson, T. (2010). *What Characteristics of Bullying, Bullying Victims, and Schools Associated with Increased Reporting of Bullying to School Officials?* Retrieved from https://files.eric.ed.gov/fulltext/ED511593.pdf.

Pipe, L. (2014). *Mental Health and Safety in Schools: Children's Perceptions and Experiences.* Electronic Thesis and Dissertation Repository, https://ir.lib.uwo.ca/etd/1931.

Plan International. (2008). *Learn Without Fear: The Global Campaign to End Violence in Schools.* Retrieved from http://www.ungei.org/Learn_Without_Fear_English.pdf.

Prall, D. (2014). *New California Law Protects Students from Cyberbullying.* Retrieved from http://americancityandcounty.com/new-laws/new-california-law-protects-students-cyberbullying.

Ramorola, M.Z., & Joyce, T.M. (2014). The links between school violence and drug usage in schools: External of internal factor? *Journal of Sociology and Social Anthropology, 5*(1), 11–18. Retrieved from http://www.krepublishers.com/02-Journals/JSSA/JSSA-05-0-000-14-Web/JSSA-05-1-000-14-Abst-PDF/JSSA-05-1-011-14-021-Ramorola-M-Z/JSSA-05-1-011-14-021-Ramorola-M-Z-Tt.pdf.

Randa, R., & Wilcox, P. (2010). Victimization, and general v. place-specific student avoidance. *Journal of Criminal Justice, 38*(2010), 854–861. DOI: 10.1016/j.crimjus.2010.05.009.

Reddy, L.A., Espelage D., McMahon, S.D., Anderman, E.M., Lane, K.L., Brown, V.E., … Kanrich, J. (2013). Violence against teachers: Case studies from the APA task force. *International Journal of School & Educational Psychology, 1*(4), 231–245. DOI: 10.1080/21683603.2013.837019.

Richardson, J. (2017). *Knocking Out School Violence and Bullying.* Retrieved from https://en.unesco.org/news/knocking-out-school-violence-and-bullying.

Rivara, F., & Le Menestrel, S. (2016). Preventing bullying through science, policy, and practice. *National Academies Press.* DOI: 10.17226/23482.

Rose, C., & Gage, N.A. (2017). Exploring the involvement of bullying among students with disabilities over time. *Exceptional Children, 83*(3), 298–314. DOI: 10.1177/0014402916667587.

Schweit, K., & Mancik, A. (2017). *School Resource Officers and Violence Prevention: Best Practices.* Retrieved from https://leb.fbi.gov/articles/featured-articles/school-resource-officers-and-violence-prevention-best-practices-part-one.

Sciberras, E., Ohan, J., & Anderson, V. (2012). Bullying and Peer Victimization in Adolescent Girls with Attention-deficit/Hyperactivity Disorder. *Child Psychiatry and Human Development, 43*(2), 254–270. DOI: 10.1007/s10578-011-0264-z.

Shen, A. (2013). *School Segregation Leads to More Violent Crime, Study Finds.* Retrieved from https://thinkprogress.org/school-segregation-leads-to-more-violen t-crime-study-finds-4b5095449e7a/.

Sherman, G. (2008). *Testing Horace Mann.* Retrieved from http://nymag.com/news/ features/45592/index3.html#print.

Sherr, L., Hensels, I.S., Skeen, S., Tomlinson, M., Roberts, K.J., & Macedo, A. (2016). Exposure to violence predicts poor educational outcomes in young children in South Africa and Malawi. *International Health, 8*(1), 36–43. DOI: 10.1093/ inthealth/ihv070.

Shetgiri, R. (2017). Bullying and children's academic performance. *Academic Pediatric Association, 17*(8), 797–798. DOI: 10.1016/j.acap.2017.08.011.

Silverberg, L. (2017). *Afterschool & Law Enforcement: Building Community between Police and Youth Recap.* Retrieved from http://www.afterschoolalliance.org/after schoolSnack/Afterschool-Law-Enforcement-Building-Community-between_09-26-2017.cfm.

Simckes, M. (2017). Guns in America: The worrying relationship between school-bullying and gun violence. Retrieved from http://www.newsweek.com/bullied-vic tims-and-gun-violence-american-schools-worrying-relationship-629752.

Simmons, R. (2011). *Odd Girl Out: The Hidden Culture of Aggression in Girls.* Boston, MA: Mariner.

Smith, P.K., & Brain, P. (2000). Bullying in schools: Lessons from two decades of research. *Aggressive Behavior, 1(26)*, 1–9. DOI: 10.1002/(SICI)1098-2337(2000)2 6:1<::AID-ABI>3.0.CO;2-7.

Steffgen, G., & Ewen, N. (2007). Teachers as victims of school violence – The influence of strain and school culture. *International Journal on Violence and Schools, 3,* 81–93. Retrieved from http://www.ijvs.org/files/Revue-03/pp-81-93-Steffgen-IJ VS-n3.pdf.

Sun, Sentinel. (2018). A history of school shootings in the United States. Retrieved from http://www.sun-sentinel.com/local/broward/parkland/florida-school-shoo ting/fl-reg-school-shooting-list-20180214-story.html.

Swearer, J.M., & Hymel, S. (2015). Understanding the psychology of bullying: Moving toward a social-ecological diathesis-stress model. *American Psychologist, 70*(4), 344–353. DOI: 10.1037/a0038929.

Temkin, D. (2012). *Giving Teachers Tools to Stop Bullying: Free Training Toolkit Now Available.* Retrieved from https://www.stopbullying.gov/blog/2012/10/05/ giving-teachers-tools-to-stop-bullying-free-training-toolkit-now-available.html.

Terry, D. (1996). *Suit Says Schools Failed to Protect a Gay Student.* Retrieved from https://www.nytimes.com/1996/03/29/us/suit-says-schools-failed-to-protect-a -gay-student.html.

Thompson, B., Mazer, J.P., Payne, H.L., Jerome, A.M., Kirby, E.G., & Pfohl, W. (2016). Social media and active shooter events: A school crisis communication challenge. *Qualitative Research Reports in Communication, 18*(1), 8 17. DOI: 10.1080/17459435.2016.1247111.

Thoreson, R. (2016). *"Like walking through a hailstorm": Discrimination against LGBT youth in US schools.* Retrieved from https://www.hrw.org/report/2016/12/07/walking-through-hailstorm/discrimination-against-lgbt-youth-us-schools.

Thrasher, F.M. (1936). *The gang: A study of 1313 gangs in Chicago.* Chicago, IL: University of Chicago Press.

Tippett, N., & Wolke, D. (2014). *Who are More Likely to be Bullies – Poor Kids or Rich Kids?* Retrieved from https://theconversation.com/who-are-more-likely-to-be-bullies-poor-kids-or-rich-kids-27411.

Tomar, D.A. (2018). *Cops in schools: Have we built a school to prison pipeline?* Retrieved from https://thebestschools.org/magazine/cops-schools-built-school-prison-pipeline/.

Trump, K. (2018). Best practices for school security and emergency preparedness planning. *National School Safety and Security Services.* Retrieved from http://www.schoolsecurity.org/trends/best-practices-for-school-security-and-emergency-preparedness-planning/.

Trump, K. (2014). School face new wave of violent threats sent by social media, and other electronic means, study says. *National School Safety and Security Services.* Retrieved from http://www.schoolsecurity.org/2014/02/schools-face-new-wave-violent-threats-sent-social-media-electronic-means-study-says/.

Twyman, K.A., Saylor, C.F., Saia, D., Macias, M.M., Taylor, L.A., & Spratt, E. (2010). Bullying and ostracism experiences in children with special health care needs. *Journal of Developmental and Behavioral Pediatrics, 31*(1), 1–8. DOI: 10.1097/DBP.0b013181c828c8.

UNICEF. (2017). *A Familiar Face: Violence in the Lives of Children and Adolescents.* Retrieved from https://www.unicefusa.org/sites/default/files/EVAClong.UN0139859.pdf.

United National Educational, Scientific, and Cultural Organization [UNESCO]. (2017). *School Violence and Bullying: Global Status Report.* Retrieved from http://unesdoc.unesco.org/images/0024/002469/246970e.pdf.

United Nations General Assembly. (2016). *Protecting Children from Bullying: Report of the Secretary-General.* Retrieved from http://srsg.violenceagainstchildren.org/sites/default/files/documents/docs/A-71-213_EN.pdf.

U.S. Department of Education, Office of Elementary and Secondary Education, Office of Safe and Healthy Students. (2013). *Guide for Developing High-Quality School Emergency Operations Plans.* Retrieved from https://rems.ed.gov/docs/REMS_K-12_Guide_508.pdf.

U.S. Department of Health and Human Services. (n.d.). *About Us.* Retrieved from https://www.stopbullying.gov/about-us/index.html.

U.S. Department of Justice: Office of Community Oriented Policing Services. (2014). *Fact Sheet: Memorandum of Understanding for School-based Partnerships.* Retrieved from https://cops.usdoj.gov/pdf/2014_MOU-FactSheet_v3_092513.pdf.

Vassallo, S., Edwards, B., Renda, J., & Olsson, C.A. (2014). Bullying in early adolescence and anti-social behavior and depression six years later: What are the protective factors? *Journal of School Violence, 13*(1), 100–124.

Volungis, A.M., & Goodman, K. (2017). School violence prevention: Teachers establishing relationships with students using counseling strategies. *SAGE,* 1–11. DOI: 10.1177/2158244017700460.

Wang, C., Berry, B., & Swearer, S.M. (2013). The critical role of school climate in effect bullying prevention. *Theory into Practice, 52*(4), 296–302. DOI: 10.1080/00405841.2012.829735.

Ward, S. (2004). *Judge Acquits Coach of Neglect.* Retrieved from https://www.thomasdamico.com/In-the-News/Judge-acquits-coach-of-neglect.shtml.

Wachtel, T. (2016). *Defining Restorative.* Retrieved from https://www.iirp.edu/images/pdf/Defining-Restorative_Nov-2016.pdf.

Weise, D. (2014). Bullying prevention: Checklist for principals. *Communicator, 37*(12). Retrieved from https://www.naesp.org/communicator-august-2014/bullying-prevention-checklist-principals.

Wells, A.S., Fox, L., & Cordova-Cobo, D. (2016). *How Radically Diverse Schools and Classrooms can Benefit all Students.* Retrieved from https://tcf.org/content/report/how-racially-diverse-schools-and-classrooms-can-benefit-all-students/?agreed=1.

Winig, L. (2015). *Making School Safe.* Retrieved from http://makingschoolsafe.com/wp-content/uploads/2015/05/MakingSchoolSafeReport.pdf.

Winn, Z. (2018). *School Security Bolstered with Omnibus Funding Bill, STOP School Violence Act.* Retrieved from https://www.campussafetymagazine.com/safety/stop-school-violence-act-security/.

Wonde, D., Jibat, N., & Baru, A. (2014). The dilemma of corporal punishment of children from parents' perspective in some selected rural and urban communities of Jimma Zone. Oromia/Ethiopia. *Global Journal of Human-Social Science: Sociology & Culture, 14*(4), 17–27. Retrieved from https://pdfs.semanticscholar.org/022a/1c9c58dd18e8998fed69afc950d16e8622dd.pdf.

Wood, M. (2018). An action plan for school safety. Retrieved from https://www.policeone.com/police-products/communications/articles/471540006-An-action-plan-for-school-safety/.

Wood, J.R. (2011). *Save the Children Afghanistan: Learning Without Fear – A Violence Free School Project Manual.* Retrieved from https://researchgate.net/publication/271327429.

Wyss, S.E. (2004). This was my 'hell': The violence experienced by gender nonconforming youth in US high schools. *International Journal of Qualitative Studies in Education, 5(17)*, 709–730. DOI: 10.1080/095183904200023676.

Zgance, A.B., Babarovic, T., Feric, I., Franc, R., Maricic, J., Merkas, M., ... Tadic, M. (2012). *2012 Croatia: External evaluation of the "For Safe and Enabling School Environment."* Retrieved from https://www.unicef.org/evaldatabase/index_69928.html.

About the Authors

Nicholas D. Young, PhD, EdD, has worked in diverse educational roles for more than thirty years, serving as a principal, special education director, graduate professor, graduate program director, graduate dean, and longtime superintendent of schools. He was named the Massachusetts Superintendent of the Year; and he completed a distinguished Fulbright program focused on the Japanese educational system through the collegiate level. Dr. Young is the recipient of numerous other honors and recognitions including the General Douglas MacArthur Award for distinguished civilian and military leadership and the Vice Admiral John T. Hayward Award for exemplary scholarship. He holds several graduate degrees including a PhD in educational administration and an EdD in educational psychology.

Dr. Young has served in the US Army and US Army Reserves combined for over thirty-four years; and he graduated with distinction from the US Air War College, the US Army War College, and the US Navy War College. After completing a series of senior leadership assignments in the US Army Reserves as the commanding officer of the 287th Medical Company (DS), the 405th Area Support Company (DS), the 405th Combat Support Hospital, and the 399th Combat Support Hospital, he transitioned to his current military position as a faculty instructor at the US Army War College in Carlisle, PA. He currently holds the rank of Colonel.

Dr. Young is also a regular presenter at state, national, and international conferences; and he has written many books, book chapters, and/or articles on various topics in education, counseling, and psychology. Some of his most recent books include *Creating Compassionate Classrooms: Expanding the Continuum of Disabilities and Effective Educational Interventions* (in-press); *Captivating Campuses: Proven Practices that Promote College Student Persistence, Engagement, and* Success (in-press); Educating *the*

Experienced: Challenges and Best Practices in Adult Learning (in-press); *Sounding the Alarm in the Schoolhouse: Safety, Security and Student Well-Being* (in-press); *The Soul of the Schoolhouse: Cultivating Student Engagement* (2019); *Embracing and Educating the Autistic Child: Valuing Those Who Color Outside the Lines* (2019); *From Cradle to Classroom: A Guide to Special Education for Young Children* (2019); *Captivating Classrooms: Student Engagement at the Heart of School Improvement* (2019); *Potency of the Principalship: Action-Oriented Leadership at the Heart of School Improvement* (2018); *Soothing the Soul: Pursuing a Life of Abundance Through a Practice of Gratitude* (2018); *Dog Tags to Diploma: Understanding and Addressing the Educational Needs of Veterans, Servicemembers, and their Families* (2018); *Turbulent Times: Confronting Challenges in Emerging Adulthood* (2018); *Guardians of the Next Generation: Igniting the Passion for Quality Teaching* (2018); *Achieving Results: Maximizing Success in the Schoolhouse* (2018); *From Head to Heart: High Quality Teaching Practices in the Spotlight* (2018); *Stars in the Schoolhouse: Teaching Practices and Approaches that Make a Difference* (2018); *Making the Grade: Promoting Positive Outcomes for Students with Learning Disabilities* (2018); *Paving the Pathway for Educational Success: Effective Classroom Interventions for Students with Learning Disabilities* (2018); *Wrestling with Writing: Effective Strategies for Struggling Students* (2018); *Floundering to Fluent: Reaching and Teaching the Struggling Student* (2018); *Emotions and Education: Promoting Positive Mental Health in Students with Learning* (2018); *From Lecture Hall to Laptop: Opportunities, Challenges, and the Continuing Evolution of Virtual Learning in Higher Education* (2017); *The Power of the Professoriate: Demands, Challenges, and Opportunities in 21st Century Higher Education* (2017); *To Campus with Confidence: Supporting a Successful Transition to College for Students with Learning Disabilities* (2017); *Educational Entrepreneurship: Promoting Public-Private Partnerships for the 21st Century* (2015); *Beyond the Bedtime Story: Promoting Reading Development during the Middle School Years* (2015); *Betwixt and Between: Understanding and Meeting the Social and Emotional Developmental Needs of Students During the Middle School Transition Years* (2014); *Learning Style Perspectives: Impact Upon the Classroom* (3rd ed., 2014); and *Collapsing Educational Boundaries from Preschool to PhD: Building Bridges Across the Educational Spectrum* (2013); *Transforming Special Education Practices: A Primer for School Administrators and Policy Makers* (2012); and *Powerful Partners in Student Success: Schools, Families and Communities* (2012). He also coauthored several children's books to include the popular series *I am Full of Possibilities*. Dr. Young may be contacted directly via email at nyoung1191@aol.com.

Christine N. Michael, PhD, is a more than 40-year educational veteran with a variety of professional experiences. She holds degrees from Brown University, Rhode Island College, Union Institute and University, and the University of Connecticut, where she earned a PhD in education, human development, and family relations. Her previous work has included middle and high school teaching, higher education administration, college teaching, and educational consulting. She has also been involved with Head Start, Upward Bound, national nonprofits Foundation for Excellent Schools and College for Every Student, and the federal Trio programs. She is currently the Program Director of Low Residency Programs at American International College.

Dr. Michael has published widely on topics in education and psychology. Her most recent works included serving as a primary author on the books *Captivating Campuses: Proven Practices that Promote College Student Persistence, Engagement, and* Success (in-press); *Sounding the Alarm in the Schoolhouse: Safety, Security and Student Well-Being* (in-press); *The Soul of the Schoolhouse: Cultivating Student Engagement* (2019); *Captivating Classrooms: Student Engagement at the Heart of School Improvement* (2019); *Turbulent Times: Confronting Challenges in Emerging Adulthood* (2018); *To Campus with Confidence: Supporting a Successful Transition to College for Students with Learning Disabilities* (2017), *Beyond the Bedtime Story: Promoting Reading Development during the Middle School Years* (2015), *Betwixt and Between: Understanding and Meeting the Social and Emotional Development Needs of Students During the Middle School Transition Years* (2014), and *Powerful Partners in Student Success: Schools, Families and Communities* (2012). Dr. Michael may be contacted via email at cnevadam@gmail.com.

Jennifer A. Smolinski, JD, has worked in education for more than three years. Her role within higher education includes the creation of, and coordinator for, the Center for Accessibility Services and Academic Accommodations at American International College located in Springfield, Massachusetts. She has also taught criminal justice and legal research and writing classes within the field of higher education. Prior to her work at the collegiate level, Attorney Smolinski worked as a solo-practitioner conducting education and disability advocacy.

Attorney Smolinski received a Bachelor of Arts in anthropology and Bachelor of Arts in sociology from the University of Connecticut, a Masters in psychology and counseling as well as a Masters of higher education/student affairs from Salem State University, and her law degree from Massachusetts School of Law. She is currently an EdD in Educational Leadership and Supervision candidate at American International College, where she is focusing her research on special education and laws to protect students with disabilities in the classroom.

Attorney Smolinski has become a regular presenter educating the faculty, staff, and students at institutes of higher education on disabilities and accommodations at the collegiate level and has presented to local high school special education departments on the transition to college under the Americans with Disabilities Act. She has coauthored *Sounding the Alarm in the Schoolhouse: Safety, Security and Student Well-Being* (in-press); *Captivating Classrooms: Student Engagement at the Heart of School Improvement* (2019); *Guardian of the Next Generation: Igniting the Passion for Quality Teaching* (2018); *Captivating Campuses: Proven Practices that Promote College Student Persistence, Engagement, and* Success (in-press); *Making the Grade: Promoting Positive Outcomes for Students with Learning Disabilities* (2018). She can be reached via email at Jennifer. Smolinski@aic.edu.